KEYWORDS FOR THE CROWLEY TAROT

KEYWORDS *for the*
CROWLEY
TAROT

Hajo Banzhaf & Brigitte Theler

WEISERBOOKS
Boston, MA/York Beach, ME

First published in 2001 by
Red Wheel/Weiser, LLC
York Beach, ME
With editorial offices at:
368 Congress Street
Boston, MA 02210
www.redwheelweiser.com

First published in German as *Schlüsselworte zum Crowley-Tarot* by Hajo Banzhaf
and Brigitte Theler (Kailash/Heinrich Hugendubel Verlag, Munich, 1998).
Copyright 1997 Hajo Banzhaf and Brigitte Theler.

Library of Congress Cataloging-in-Publication Data:

Banzhaf, Hajo
  [German Schlüsselworte zum Crowley-Tarot, English]
  Keywords for the Crowley Tarot / Hajo Banzhaf, Brigitte Theler
  p.   cm.
  Includes bibliographical references.
  ISBN 1-57863-173-4 (pbk. : alk. paper)
  1. Tarot. I. Theler, Brigitte. II. Title
BF1870.T2 B3413   2001
133.3'2424—dc21   00--47315
                                         CIP

Translated from the German by Christine Grimm
Typeset in 10/12 Adobe Garamond

Cover design by Kathryn Sky-Peck
Illustrations on the cover are The Universe, The Chariot, The Aeon, and The Art
major tarot trumps from the Crowley Thoth Deck. Illustrations in the text are
from the Crowley Thoth Deck published by Weiser Books.

Printed in the United States of America
VG
08 07 06 05 04
9 8 7 6 5 4 3 2

Contents

WHAT IS
THE TAROT?

The Origin of the Tarot

T he tarot is a card oracle that has existed in its current form since the 16th century. The deck consists of 78 cards, which are subdivided into two main groups: the major arcana,[1] which consists of 22 consecutively numbered cards depicting individual motifs, such as the Fool, the Magus, the Sun and Moon, as well as Death and the Devil. The remaining 56 cards, the minor arcana, are arranged into a series of four suits. Each suit displays a common symbol (Wand, Sword, Disk, or Cup).

There are many differing opinions as to where this oracle came from and how it originally reached Europe. The earliest traces are lost in the 14th century. It is presumed that this is the time when the minor arcana came to the West from the Islamic world. On the other hand, the origin of the considerably more significant cards of the major arcana is uncertain. They only appeared around the end of the 16th century. It is not known whether the connection with the minor arcana first occurred at that time or whether all 78 cards had always belonged together.

Many people believe that these cards are nothing less than the ancient Egyptian priest caste's Book of Wisdom, which had blossomed in the dark for several thousands of years until they reached the light of public life about 400 years ago. However, others assume that the cards were created in the 14th century, which is undoubtedly the more plausible assumption.

As mysterious as the origin of the major arcana may be, its "disappearance" is also quite curious. Even though almost everyone is familiar with the minor arcana, because our current playing cards are based on it, only The Fool of the major arcana has "survived." He became the Joker. The other 21 cards disappeared from the card games that are commonly played today. Yet the four suits of the minor arcana, including their structure, are still found in our playing cards. The symbols—Wands, Swords, Cups, and Coins—which are widespread in card games from Roman-influenced countries even today, have now become Clubs, Spades, Hearts, and Diamonds.

Two Approaches to the Tarot

There are basically two different ways to approach the tarot. If we study the symbolism, the organization, and the structure of the cards, the images of the major arcana become a Book of Wisdom. They describe the human being's path of life and also permit meaningful insight into the reality behind reality. This deeply esoteric approach to the tarot is limited to the 22 cards of the major arcana, which

---

[1] From the Latin *arcanum* = "secret," *arcana* = "secrets."

form the actual philosophical background and contain the tarot's wisdom about life. Above all, important keys to this profound level are found in mythology,[2] alchemy, and mystical numerology. In comparison, we do not know whether the cards of the minor arcana have ever been used for any other purpose than card-laying, which is the second, much more familiar way of approaching the tarot. And it is also the topic of this book. On this level, the differences between the major and minor arcana fade since they are treated almost the same when it comes to using the cards in a reading.

Coincidence and the Random Oracle

The relationship between an oracle and a game is not a phenomenon limited to the tarot cards. Other games we play, such as throwing dice, drawing lots, or Mikado, have also descended from ancient oracles. They are all based on the conviction that coincidence is something meaningful. Although the statement, "There are no coincidences," that we often hear today may mean the same thing, a closer look reveals its fallacy. We should actually say that there are no meaningless coincidences. That would correspond more closely with the original meaning of this word in the Middle Ages, which is based on the idea of "coinciding" or two things occurring at the same time. The philosophers of the European "Enlightenment" in the 18th century liked the approach that coincidences were purely arbitrary, depicting an absurd fate or the blind workings of life. This helped them through the embarrassing predicament of having to find explanations for inexplicable phenomena. However, our present-day willingness to presume a significant activity behind a coincidence or synchronicity has increased considerably. What does this mean?

When we translate our philosophy about our path to salvation (as described in a great variety of humanity's spiritual teachings) into the language of psychology, then our goal in life is to achieve wholeness. The force that urges each of us to strive for this goal is the "Self." C. G. Jung used this term to describe the greater whole that encompasses both conscious and unconscious aspects of a human being. Since our ego, as the center of consciousness, is only a part of the Self—and with great probability just a very small portion—it naturally cannot develop an extensive view of the greater whole. Neither can it speak with certainty about the nature of the Self.

However, we can pay attention to the messages it sends us via dream and inspiration. We can also observe its activity in the many coincidental phenomena of our lives. Similar to the situation of subtle quantum physics, the observer is nat-

---

2 Also see Hajo Banzhaf's *Tarot and the Journey of the Hero,* a study of the mythological key to the major arcana, also published by Weiser.

urally a part of the experiment as well. If we think that dreams are just nonsense, our dreams will hardly have anything meaningful to say to us. But if we pay friendly attention to the inspiration coming from the unconscious mind, as well as to coincidental occurrences, we will notice some unusual and memorable experiences.

From this perspective, we know that oracles make significant statements, especially because of their random patterns, even if making such an assumption is blatantly contrary to the scientific way of looking at things. And here is where we repeatedly hear judgments in relation to reading the tarot: "If the cards are laid out five times in a row, an answer is given through different cards each time." This is both true and false. Actually, in such a situation, different cards would actually turn up, but this doesn't prove anything. Only the rational presentation of evidence is based on the repeatability of an experiment. To do this, it is necessary to exclude coincidences with a vengeance, to carry out a planned test series without any disturbances in an appropriate room, a shielded laboratory, for instance. If the experiment succeeds as many times as desired, proof has been provided. However, random oracles, just like dreams, belong to the irrational world, and therefore cannot be measured with such rational means.

A dream doesn't first become meaningful when we have dreamed it five times. In the same way, a random oracle does not live from its repeatability. While coincidence is considered an unknown quantity and an undesired troublemaker that can confuse any experiment in the rational world, it proves to be the most important and expressive factor in the irrational world. This is why the pattern of an initial and single laying of the cards is meaningful. The fact that it cannot be repeated does not prove anything.

If we consider Jungian psychology and assume that forces found in the unconscious mind guide us, then the tarot can also symbolize a dialog between the conscious and the unconscious mind. Just like the other occurrences and experiences that are brought about by the unconscious mind so we can grow and mature, advice from the tarot also comes into our lives with messages from the unconscious mind. This background allows the oracle to appear in a completely different light and become a unique source of self-perception. So that it would be understood in this way, the philosopher Thales of Miletus had the famous inscription of "Know thyself," written on the Temple at Delphi at the beginning of the sixth century B.C. to explain the actual meaning of all oracles. People who comprehend these messages, and who allow themselves to be guided by them, will take their very own path, one that corresponds with their individuality, and they will find themselves as a result. On the other hand, those who consider the unconscious mind to be nothing more than an enchanted wonderland with magical powers that the ego may shamelessly exploit in order to satisfy its boundless craving for recognition and naive expectations of happiness, will at best be disappointed. People who want to learn their numbers to play the lottery, or who consider the tarot as spiritual insurance against the inconveniences of life, may not be very successful. "Every approach to the unconscious, or just wanting to make use of it," warns the Jungian Marie-Louise von Franz, "has destructive effects."[3] And she compares this process to the ruthless exploitation of the forests, the ruinous exhaustion of natural resources, and the greedy plundering of our mineral resources—all of which only leads to a disturbance of the biological equilibrium. Moreover, missing the point is the original meaning of the word "sin." Perhaps it is this danger that, time and again, has discredited the tarot cards as the prayerbook of the Devil.

---

[3]Marie-Louise von Franz, *Individuation in Fairy Tales* (Boston: Shambhala, 1990), p. 36.

VARIOUS VERSIONS
OF THE TAROT

The Traditional Cards

Theere are many variations of the tarot common today, but the Marseilles Tarot is considered to be the most classic version because it is most closely related to the card motifs of past centuries. Yet, we still cannot say that this is the original depiction, since the cards have always proved to have a great degree of variation between them, and no original tarot is known. A typical characteristic of older cards is that only the major arcana, the court cards (King, Queen, Knight, and Page) and sometimes also the four Aces have picture motifs. Apart from ornamental flourishes and garlands, the illustrations on the remaining cards are essentially limited to the numerical rendition of their symbol, similar to present-day playing cards. For example, the Five of Coins shows 5 coins, just like the Five of Diamonds shows 5 diamonds. It is understandably much more difficult to interpret these cards. We must either learn all their meanings by heart, or use another system to find the message of each card.

One way to increase our knowledge is to classify the four suits of the minor arcana according to the four elements: Wands = fire, Swords = air, Coins = earth, and Cups = water. If we also consider the knowledge of the meaning of the numbers 1 to 10, passed down by mystical numerology, the meaning of a card can be derived from these two components. Since, among other things, the number 3 represents healthy stability and living growth, and Cups are equivalent to the water element and the world of feelings, the following meaning results from the Three of Cups: feeling healthy and full of life. Without a doubt, such an approach to the cards is more difficult and less inspiring for most people than working with an expressive picture.

The Waite Tarot

At the beginning of the 20th century, Arthur Edward Waite (1857–1942) and Pamela Coleman Smith (1875–1951) created new cards. These were published in 1910 as the Waite Tarot, or the Rider-Waite Tarot,[1] and became the best-known tarot cards in the world, and have the broadest distribution. Both creators of these cards were members of the Order of the Golden Dawn, an esoteric society that was London's most famous at the turn of the 19th century. This circle, which included many illustrious personalities as its members, was extremely interested in the Western tradition and tarot in particular. A. E. Waite, who was also the head of the order

---

[1]William Rider & Co. was the original publisher of these cards in London, which is why we call them the Rider-Waite deck. It is more correct to call it the Waite deck.

at times, was considered the "walking library" of the house. On the basis of his deep and extensive knowledge, he created the concept for the new cards. The artist Pamela Coleman Smith turned this concept into the pictures on the cards. While the depiction of the major arcana usually reflected the classical patterns, the minor arcana was given a completely new design. Each minor arcana card was illustrated, making it possible to derive the meaning of all 78 cards from the motifs. This change contained such an enormous enrichment for the cards that it has been the main reason for their great popularity.

The Crowley Tarot

Second today in terms of popularity—at least in English- and German-speaking areas—is a tarot deck created by the highly controversial Aleister Crowley (1875–1947), who many people denounce as a magician who practiced black magic, while others—including some very clever minds—see him as one of the great initiates. Crowley, who in his childhood suffered from the sectarian narrowness of his parental home and was not allowed to experience Christianity as a message of love, had passionately proclaimed the end of this world religion and claimed that he was the Anti-Christ, ultimately even the prophet of a new age. Since he fanned all the Christian fears that had been slumbering since the Middle Ages in the people of the Western world, and because he also rarely missed an opportunity to make himself unpopular, Crowley was not only stamped an arch villain but also fell lastingly into disrepute, far beyond his own age, so that even today some faint-hearted souls flinch at the sound of his name. More than a few people fear that becoming interested in his work is a certain ticket to Hell. That is not true.

Crowley was neither a criminal nor did he propagandize evil. He was concerned with defeating a belief that, in his eyes, was outdated and hypocritical. However, for this purpose he had the audacity of besmirching the holy values of the Western world. He has never been forgiven for this insolence. Since his attempt to establish a new world religion has remained rather unsuccessful, and his magic only interests a relatively small circle of ardent insiders, the name Crowley would have long been forgotten except for one fact: toward the end of his life he developed a new tarot. This tarot was first published in 1944 as *The Book of Thoth*, named after the ancient Egyptian god of wisdom and magic spells. He let all his magical knowledge flow into these cards, which were painted by the artist Lady Frieda Harris (1887–1962). And since he was a highly educated, widely traveled man, and extraordinarily well-versed authority of esoteric tradition, it is no wonder that this tarot deck not only fascinates us but has also remained unsurpassed to this day in its symbolic content and complexity.

In contrast to the Waite Tarot, these exceedingly profound images present a problem. Although the pictures are fascinating, they are not simple and pleasing. Particularly because of the depth and abundance of their symbolism, it is not always easy to gain access to their meaning. A further factor is that in the design of the minor arcana, Crowley places himself between the simple but shallow depiction of the old cards and the easily understandable motifs of the Waite Tarot. We could say that he abstracted the respective idea in his cards. As a result, their meaning is expressed quite well, but only for those who are capable of reading the symbols. As if to balance out this complication a bit, each card of the Crowley Tarot has a name. For some, this may be a helpful bridge to interpretation. However, some people simply read the name without exploring the picture, which is known to say more than a thousand words. As a result, they only get a vague idea (or none at all) of what the card would truly like to express.

The Crowley Tarot is different in structure from the Waite deck. This difference has caused confusion for Crowley changed the names of the Court cards, which overlap with the old names in the following, easily misunderstood manner:

Traditional names of the Court cards	Corresponding Court cards in the Crowley Tarot
King	Knight
Queen	Queen
Knight	Prince
Page	Princess

Furthermore, some of the cards in the major arcana of the Crowley Tarot received new names. Justice became Adjustment (VIII); while the Wheel of Fortune was shortened to Fortune (X); Strength became Lust (XI); Temperance was transformed into Art (XIV); The World is called The Universe (XXI). But the most fundamental change occurred in the 20th card. It has been called Judgement and showed the wonder of resurrection on the Day of Judgment. According to Crowley's understanding, this theme belonged to the closing age of Osiris, the age of the sacrificed and self-sacrificing gods. But his newly designed card, The Aeon, is devoted to the approaching age of Horus,[2] upon which Horus can be seen as the ruler of this new eon. This approach naturally also transforms the meaning of this card. It no longer represents redemption and the wonder of transformation, as in the older tarots, but the birth of the new and the vision of a broad future.

Some people who have copies of the newer small Crowley deck will note that there are two extra copies of the Magus. When the deck was rephotographed in the 1980s, the photographer discovered two other versions of the card and

---

[2]The terms, which Crowley chose, correspond thematically to the Age of Pisces (Osiris) and the dawning Age of Aquarius (Horus).

arranged to have them printed with the deck. However, these are not cards meant to be in the deck; they were reprinted in error and should not be included. They were not "special cards" to be used in readings, but were actually paintings that were rejected by Crowley. The card manufacturer has now stopped including them in the deck as they should never have been included in the first place. No one, for example, publishes the card designs that "didn't make it" in the Waite deck!

Other Tarot Variations

What some people experience as a qualitative enrichment appears to others to be one of the many inflations of our age as it thirsts for quantity: the constantly increasing and hardly surveyable number of new tarot cards. The spectrum ranges from countless variations of the Waite deck and classical tarots, to peculiar curiosities and supposed exotics, to beautiful new editions of old decks and to many decks with romantic titles, which their creators like to name after sunken cultures or mysterious figures. A closer look usually reveals that even the "Far Eastern," "Traditional," and "Ancient Egyptian" tarots have only been created during recent decades in Europe or the USA.

Are There Right and Wrong Tarot Cards?

In view of this development, we can question whether or not and to what degree it can be right for an increasing number of new tarot decks to be created, today more than ever before. At the same time, rumors circulate as to the existence of cards that are especially good and reliable, whereby other cards—like the works of the Devil—harm the users and lead them astray. But whether a tarot deck is right or wrong depends on what we do with the cards. If we study them as a Book of Wisdom (see page 3), we can quickly determine whether the symbolism of the major arcana has been understood by those who gave them the new design and perhaps even enriched them with a few subtle nuances. They will reveal whether the core message has been retained or falsified. On the other hand, if we lay the cards to ask them questions as an oracle, then there is no right or wrong. The decisive factor is not which tarot is used, or whether an answer is obtained from reading the runes, the I Ching, or coffee grounds. What matters is how well-versed the reader is in the language of the respective oracle, or how well the asker understands the message that has been laid by coincidence in the corresponding arrangement. There are oracle systems that have matured during the course of the centuries and can therefore give a more highly differentiated answer than simpler methods, such as throwing a coin. And when someone designs a tarot deck that only has a choice of dark themes, the answer will inevitably be one-sided; the same applies to a tarot deck that consists solely of harmlessly sweet motifs.

Frequently Asked Questions and Answers

What can you ask the cards?

- About the current status of a matter or development
- About future tendencies and perspectives
- For advice on how to solve a problem or achieve a goal
- About the causes and reasons for a specific development
- About the best decision or smartest course of action
- About issues regarding self-awareness or self-realization

What can't we learn from the cards?

Cards can only pictorially depict a theme; they cannot present us with names or places. They obviously won't give us telephone numbers, dates, and times. They are also not capable of medical diagnosis. But, above all, they cannot answer with "yes" or "no." If you are seeking this type of advice, it is better to try throwing coins. However, the cards can help in making such decisions by showing the consequences without making the decision for the person asking the question.

How can the cards give us meaningful answers?

This phenomenon certainly cannot be adequately explained. However, there are two interesting considerations beyond the information in the chapter on "Coincidence and the Random Oracle."

1. The unconscious mind has a different relationship to time and space than the conscious mind. It looks beyond the horizons of the present, as everyone has experienced in dreaming about the future and knowing what is about to happen. Just as the language of consciousness is words, the unconscious mind speaks in images. The tarot cards can be understood as the alphabet of the metaphorical language of our soul. With them, our unconscious mind can express how it sees the matter in question. The only thing that our conscious mind must do is learn the metaphorical language of the unconscious to understand what it is saying.

2. The second consideration underlies the concept of synchronicity, as C. G. Jung has termed this phenomenon. We are used to measuring time in terms of quantity. There is, however, also a quality of time that our language remembers when it speaks of the "right" moment. And from this perspective, every moment has its special quality and characteristics that reveal themselves on a great variety of levels in the same way: macrocosmic in the planetary constellations, microcosmic in the movements of the atoms, and on many other different levels in between. These other levels include the tarot, as well as the I Ching and other oracle methods. Since, from the holistic perspective, the question and its answer form a unity, the

moment in which we ask the question already contains the answer. If we succeed in recognizing the quality of this moment, we can read the answer from it. The question of which oracle to use or which tarot cards are better is less significant. Above all, it is important that the interpreter understands the language of the oracle.

Is there a secret, but really true, final, and objective meaning for the cards?

No. There are only subjective interpretations. This is why there are very different, sometimes even highly contradictory statements in the books and interpretations of various, quite competent experts. One reason for this is that the tarot is not a secret language thought up by a sage or a group of initiates at some point in time, the code of which we now must crack. Instead, these are archetypal symbols—particularly in the cards of the major arcana—that correspond to and originate in the picture language of the soul. Consequently, the key is to be found much less in the mysterymongering of some occult circles than in the depth psychology of C. G. Jung. In keeping with its nature, a symbol can never be understood to mean just one thing or comprehended in all its depth. In this respect, even very different interpretations can be correct, since each of them respectively illuminates another aspect of the whole.

How can it be that the asker draws the "right" cards without knowing what they mean or which card-laying system the interpreter will use?

The basic rule is: "The asker always plays the game of the interpreter." On the unconscious level, we are much more connected with each other than our external impression would have us believe. This means that something like a state of unity occurs between two participants, thanks to which the asker draws the right card for the respective interpreter. In this regard, it also makes no sense to have the interpretation "appraised" by another person with knowledge of the cards, since the asker would possibly have drawn other cards for this person's insight. Yet, the cards would have still led to the same message.

What differences in quality are there when people interpret the cards?

The quality of the interpretation is naturally dependent upon the interpreter's inner horizon. Those who live with a limited worldview will only be able to translate the cards within the confines of their imagination. On the other hand, the asker's level of understanding is always dependent upon his or her degree of maturity. If we only want to know when we will finally get lucky, whether something will turn out well, or when something unpleasant will finally be over, without being interested in the deeper reasons, we will perhaps be particularly disappointed by a truly sound and competent consultation because it doesn't give us a simple answer.

*Should you concentrate on the question while
shuffling, picking, drawing, or laying the cards?*

No, definitely not. Let yourself be guided by the concept that your unconscious mind already knows what you want to ask. Your conscious mind just needs to know what the question is. In this respect, asking the question is nothing other than becoming aware of it and should also be seen in this light. So be clear about what you would like to know. While you shuffle, draw, or lay the cards, it may be that you have almost forgotten what the question was (which is why it is better to write it down so you can again focus on it during the interpretation).

What should you keep in mind when shuffling the cards?

This depends upon how you want to proceed. If you follow the advice of this book and draw each card individually from the cards of the tarot deck that have been turned face down and spread like a fan, then shuffling is insignificant. You don't need to give it any further thought. On the other hand, if you simply lay the cards that are at the top of the mixed pile, you should actually observe the mixing ritual described by some books so that you mix (or shuffle) the "right" cards to be in that place.

   If you also read the "reversed" cards (see page 27), it is advisable to mix the cards with both hands on the large surface, such as a table or desk so that these have the opportunity to turn in one direction or the other.

*How do you know which of the many meanings
of a card are correct in each individual case?*

From your intuition. You should not be surprised if you—as the interpreter—suddenly emphasize a previously neglected aspect or discover a whole new aspect of a card. Instead, be rather skeptical if you continually recite the same set interpretation. However, if it happens that you are stuck at some point without a clue, the cards themselves can also help you get further. Ask about the special meaning of a card by laying The Cross (see page 51).

*If you lay the cards on the same topic several times
in a row, will the same cards appear again?*

Probably not. Whether or not laying the cards a number of times actually expresses a message depends upon the reason for laying them again. If someone just wants to use this to prove the supposed nonsense of laying cards at all, then laying them repeatedly is meaningless (also see the chapter on "Coincidence and the Random Oracle"). The same also applies to the case when the asker is dissatisfied with the first laying and therefore immediately draws the cards again. However, if this is a matter of clarifying one or more subsequent questions regarding the interpretation at hand, experience has shown that further card-laying consistently builds upon the previous one without getting "tangled up" in contradictions.

For which period of time are the cards reliable?
For which time periods can you ask questions of the cards?

This depends completely on the time factor associated with the question. Generally, the cards provide an outlook for the next three to six months. However, if you ask about a change of residence or a different direction in your work, the cards can illuminate a much longer period of time. On the other hand, if you ask about a two-week vacation period, they will be limited to this time frame.

In addition, some cards have a time aspect of their own: the Eight of Wands and sometimes The Chariot (VII) show a shortening of the required time aspect. By way of contrast, the Eight of Disks and, above all, the Four of Swords and The Hanged Man (XII) sometimes reflect considerable delays in the development of the matter in question.

How reliable is the card oracle?

As reliable as the advice of the wise old man or woman. Therefore, take the message of the cards seriously and take their recommendations to heart. But since absolute truth cannot be found in this world, it naturally does not exist in the tarot either.

The cards—like all other oracles—point out experiences that we will have. In this respect, their statements are very reliable. But how we react to these experiences and what events are related to them cannot be predicted with certainty beforehand. This applies in particular to people who live in a very conscious manner and who don't switch to a comfortable hypocritical solution when faced with difficult challenges. They shape their freedom of development within such a broad scope that the "hits" of prognosis are far below the level of those for people who live unconsciously for the most part. The latter tend to give themselves over to their fate and take the path of least resistance. Consequently, they react in a much more predictable manner.

In any case, you should assume that no one session of card-laying is binding, but instead shows a tendency that will occur if the asker continues in the same way as before. However, even if someone just takes a different approach on the basis of the perspectives shown by the tarot, the tendency that the cards have predicted is naturally no longer applicable.

Is there a limit to the possible messages and therefore
things that a card-reader cannot or should not predict?

Yes. In contradiction to the common conceptions, a card-reader is not a fortune-teller but a translator who speaks the language of the images. This makes the card-reader like an interpreter of dreams. The meaning of the message can be found in conveying a deeper understanding for the larger context of a current or future development. From worthless to questionable are messages that go beyond that and announce a seemingly inescapable event.

Is it possible to become addicted to the tarot?

There are certainly people who will not take a step before asking the cards for permission. But they have not become dependent because of the tarot—they presumably have an addictive personality structure that could have just as easily latched onto something else. Fortunately, tarot addiction is one of the few addictions that can cure itself. While other addictions constantly call for more and increase their intensity as a result, this addiction fades with time because the more wildly the cards are laid, the more their expressive power is watered down to the point of meaninglessness.

Could it be that the cards or other oracles manipulate the asker? Does he or she perhaps have a negative experience only because its occurrence was predicted?

This occurrence naturally cannot be excluded with certainty, which is why it is important each time before laying the cards to ask whether you are truly willing to hear *any* answer. If you let other people give you advice, be sure that they are people who you experience as likable and trustworthy; avoid any dark, threatening advice that sheds no light on your life.

How should you deal with predictions of disaster?

Time and again people have seen fortune-tellers who apparently set no limits on the messages they give, who supposedly have prophesied unavoidable misfortune (death of close relatives, financial ruin followed by suicide, etc.). A discussion on how such statements are arbitrary and untenable then has little effect. It is only when the asker understands that he or she "needs" this prophecy, possibly to take a new look at his or her partner, that the emotional pressure is eased. (This is the issue at hand since the prophesied apocalypse doesn't occur at any rate.) This is in no way meant to justify the fact that irresponsible fortune-tellers make unfounded and terrible statements that are also worthless.[3] Yet, it is important to understand that the asker, as in any other consultation or therapy, receives exactly the message or experience that he or she probably "needs" for the respective situation.

What is the meaning of the oracle?

Its significance is found in the search for self-awareness and not in the prediction

---

[3]Even if it would be possible to make a statement about the way in which a person will die, and even if this statement would be accurate, it would still be completely worthless because this knowledge would not serve the asker in any way nor promote his or her self-awareness.

of profane everyday events. What makes the tarot (as well as astrology and the I Ching) so valuable is the deep understanding of our tasks in life and the nature of our being, to which each of these oracles would like to lead us and can do so.

What is the relationship between tarot and astrology or the I Ching?

While the strength of the tarot is in clearly showing developments in close proximity, astrology is an excellent key to our nature as human beings, our tasks in life, and our larger cycles of experience. Above all, the I Ching may give valuable insights to those who desire to penetrate into a deeper level of meaning in relation to an experience.

Each of these oracles speaks its own language, but the Western traditions of tarot and astrology are closely related to each other. Their relationship is something like English and German: they can easily be translated from one to the other. Yet, there are still expressions in both languages that can only be described in the other. On the other hand, the distance to the I Ching is as great as the difference between English and Chinese. A deep intuitive understanding of the other culture is required in order to understand its language.

Should the cards even be asked questions about everyday life?

Yes, of course. Any question that an individual seriously asks can also be asked of the tarot.

Can you lay the cards for someone who is not present?

Yes, you can, as long as you have this person's permission and/or have a justifiable interest. The latter case occurs, for example, if you have a relationship with a person and lay the cards in order to ask something about the status of this relationship. However, if someone attempts to snoop in the private life of another person because of curiosity or sensation-seeking, without the other person's permission, the statements made by the cards are usually worthless.

Why are the cards drawn with the left hand?

Because, in pictorial terms, it comes from the heart and the left half of the body has always been considered the intuitive side. This knowledge has been confirmed by the latest brain research. Left-handers should also draw their cards with the left hand.

Should you let your cards be drawn by someone else?

Yes, you should, if you have a great deal of inner tension or expectations that are too fixed in connection with the question. Then it is definitely better to have the cards drawn, laid, and interpreted by someone you like.

FROM ASKING THE QUESTION
TO INTERPRETING
THE ANSWER

Quick Access for People in a Hurry

I f you are too impatient to read long instructions and prefer to start immediately, or simply want to try out how to lay the cards, then proceed as follows:

1. Ask a question about a topic that interests you. If this happens to be a decision question, don't formulate the question so that it can only be answered with "yes" or "no." Instead, ask what will happen if you do something and what will happen if you don't do it.

2. Look for the appropriate card-laying system in Table 1 on page 22. If you find this too confusing, then use one of the three following methods for laying the cards:

   a) The Relationship Game (page 40) for questions about a relationship

   b) The Decision Game (page 44) for all questions regarding decisions

   c) The Celtic Cross (page 48) for all other questions.

3. Shuffle all 78 tarot cards and spread them out facedown like a fan in front of you.

4. Look at the description to see how many cards you will need for the card-laying system that you have selected.

5. Place the cards in front of you in a fan shape. Draw each card, one at a time, using you left hand. Don't concentrate or think of anything in particular. Place the cards facedown on top of each other.

6. Now turn over one card after the other in the order you drew it (meaning the bottom one first). Lay them out according to the numerical order given in the description of the card-laying method.

7. Read the keywords for each card on the respective level of your question in the interpretation section and meaningfully connect these with the significance of the place that the card occupies.

8. Connect the individual statements with each other into an overall message.

9. In conclusion, find the Quintessence (see page 28).

Table 1. Card-Laying Systems According to Question and Degree of Difficulty.

CARD-LAYING SYSTEM	MESSAGE	DIFFICULTY
The Ankh	Causes, backgrounds, and thematic tendencies	4
The Astrological Tarot Reading	Extensive description of present and future tendencies	4
The Relationship Game	Status of relationship between two people	2
The Blind Spot	Self-knowledge	3
The Decision Game	Two possible tendencies, help in decision-making	2
The Secret of the High Priestess	Course of a situation and its hidden meaning	3
The Card for the Year	Theme for the coming year	0
The Celtic Cross	Tendencies—suitable for all questions	2
The Cross	Evaluation of a situation; suggestions and trends	1
The Next Step	What should be done next?	1
The Fool's Game	Current position and long-term perspectives	4
The Partner Game	How partners relate to each other	1
The Plan Game	Suggestion for achieving a goal	1
Pro and Con	Quick help in decision-making	1
The Card for the Day	Tendency for the day	0
The Door	Pictorial description of the threshold at which we stand	4
The Path	The best approach to achieve a goal	3

How Should the Question Be Asked?

In Terms of Its Form:

You can ask the question aloud or quietly, repeat it several times, or even write it down. Do this in whatever way appeals to you most. No method is better than the other. The important thing is that you know precisely what you have asked and that you no longer concentrate on the question after you have asked it. Instead, calmly and serenely draw the cards, turn them over, and interpret them.

In Terms of Its Content:

Consider your question as it comes to mind; the important thing is not a perfect formulation, but that you are clear about what you want to know. So you can simply ask: "What is the situation for this or that?" or, "How will things continue?" You can also check the "Typical Questions" at the beginning of each layout to help you find the best method for your question.

Don't ask questions that can only be answered with "yes" or "no." It's quite possible that the cards will help you in decision-making situations, but they cannot make any decisions for you. Instead, ask: "What will happen if I do this, and what will happen if I don't do this?" The Decision Game will show you the respective consequences, which will help you make your decision.

Don't ask about a number of alternatives at the same time, such as: "Should I move to New York or to Paris?" Instead, divide your query into two sets of questions: "What will happen if I go to New York," and "What will happen if I don't go to New York?" Actually, with Decision Game layout, you can combine these two questions in one reading. After you have asked these questions, you can ask: "What will happen if I move to Paris?" and "What will happen if I don't move to Paris?" If the prospects are bleak in both cases, but the cards show a more favorable alternative, this may perhaps be Los Angeles. But in the original formulation of the question, you would have not even been aware of this alternative. It would only have shown you that your plans were problematic either way.

Various groups of themes should not be mixed into one question, such as: "How will my vacation trip be and will I fall in love along the way?" Instead, ask how the vacation will be by using the card-laying system "The Celtic Cross" and try "The Path" to see what you can do to fall in love again.

Shuffling, Drawing, and Laying the Cards

After you have asked the question and decided which card-laying system to use, proceed as follows:

1. Shuffle the cards. You don't need to pay attention to any special rules. Mix them as long as you like and however you like.

2. Spread the cards in front of you like a big fan.

3. With your left hand, draw as many cards from the fan as you need for the selected card-laying method. Lay them on top of each other, facedown, and one at a time.

4. Set aside the rest of the cards.

5. Now turn over your cards in the order you drew them (which means the bottom one first) and lay them out according to the pattern shown in the illustration of the respective card-laying system you have chosen to use.

THE INTERPRETATION

The Individual Cards

W|hen interpreting the cards, it's important to connect the special meaning of each card with the meaning of the field in which it is located. You will find the meaning of the field in the description of the respective card-laying system. You can then look up the various levels of meaning of the card in the Interpretation Section. Look for the key word that corresponds with your question and combine it into a meaningful message together with the meaning of the field where the card is located.

When you first start reading the cards, it is quite common at the start for the individual messages to be clumsy, or not particularly expressive or understandable. Don't let yourself be disappointed by this. Simply move on to the next card. At the conclusion, the meaning of the less understandable cards usually becomes more clear.

In some card-laying systems, it is helpful to interpret the cards in an order different from how they were picked from the deck. You will find corresponding suggestions under the heading of "How to Interpret the Cards," for each different spread.

Summarizing the Message

A summary of the message should be done at the end of each reading. To do this, connect the individual statements into an overall message. However, this doesn't mean that all the contradictions must be rigorously cleared away. Our lives—and therefore also the cards—are frequently quite contradictory. The interpretation should not be just bits and pieces, but summarized into a concluding message. So let the individual elements become a complete story.

Reversed Cards

Some experts see a different meaning in the cards when they are reversed (upside down). Others simply turn the cards back to the right position. Both approaches are correct and simply depend, like so many things in tarot, on the "rules of the game" that the interpreter uses. Try this variation and see what your experiences are with it. But always decide before you draw the first card whether or not you want to use reversed meanings. If you do, be sure to mix the cards on a large surface (such as a table) so that they actually have the opportunity to get really mixed up. Since Brigitte and I always turn reversed cards to the proper position, we have not included interpretative text for reversed cards in this book. However, you may find that reversed cards have a problematic, exaggerated, or complicated variation of their original meanings. Other books list specific meanings for reversed cards, and you may want to explore that as well.

The Quintessence

After the cards have been laid and interpreted, the tarot can give an additional indication of how the asker should deal with the cards' advice and what should be taken into special consideration in future actions. You can calculate the quintessence by adding the numerical value of the cards that have been turned over. In this process, the Court cards (Princess, Prince, Queen, and Knight) have a value of zero, the aces are ones, and the remaining cards are added according to their numerical value.

If this results in a single-digit number, then look for the card of the major arcana that corresponds with this number. It will show you the proper course of action. However, if the result is a two-digit or three-digit number, then add the cross sum[1] until you have a single-digit number. Should the sum or the cross sum first result in a double-digit number between 10 and 22, the corresponding card of the major arcana will give you additional information. It may even be a precondition for coming to the actual theme that is always found in the single-digit cards. You can find the meaning of the quintessence in the overview provided in Table 2 on pages 28–30.

Table 2. The Quintessence.

Number	Card	Advice
1	The Magus	Take the initiative. Approach things actively. Skillfully master your task.
2	The High Priestess	Be ready. Let yourself be guided. Trust that your inner voice will tell you what you should do and when you should do it.
3	The Empress	You are walking on fertile ground. Trust in the life force. Ponder the matter.
4	The Emperor	Consider the matter in a sober and realistic way. Create order and be sure not to lose the red thread. Be persistent and determined, but flexible. as you turn your plans into reality.
5	The Hierophant	Don't cling to exoteric or dead forms. Look for the hidden meaning. Let yourself be guided by deep conviction.

[1]The cross sum results by adding together the digits of a number. The cross sum of 365, for example, is 3 + 6 + 5 = 14; the new cross sum is then 1 + 4 = 5.

Table 2. The Quintessence (cont.).

Number	Card	Advice
6	The Lovers	Make a decision of the heart. Take a loving approach and pay attention to what you have in common with others and what connects you.
7	The Chariot	Concentrate on your goal and set out immediately.
8	Adjustment	Weigh things carefully. Make a sensible and well-considered decision. Be aware that you are personally responsible for everything else that may result.
9	The Hermit	Retreat within yourself to find out what you really want. Don't let yourself be influenced.
10/1	Fortune/ The Magus	Recognize a portion of your task in life in the theme of the question. The time has come to dedicate yourself to this matter (Fortune). You now have the strength and the skill to master the related tasks (The Magus).
11/2	Lust/The High Priestess	Show your desire and approach this topic with passion (Lust), completely trusting that your inner voice (The High Priestess) will guide you in the decisive moment.
12/3	The Hanged Man/ The Empress	The matter has become bogged down. It will only blossom after a fundamental reversal or a new evaluation (The Hanged Man) and grow in a lively way (The Empress).
13/4	Death/The Emperor	An old structure must be ended (Death) so that a new structure can arise (The Emperor).
14/5	Art/The Hierophant	Seek the proper mixture. Despite all the tensions, attempt to connect opposites with each other. Go into the depths (Art), then you will understand the meaning of the whole (The Hierophant).
15/6	The Devil/ The Lovers	Perceive your concealed motivations. Bring light into the darkness. Free yourself from dependencies (The Devil) so that you can take the path of the heart's free decision (The Lovers).

Table 2. The Quintessence (cont).

Number	Card	Advice
16/7	The Tower/ The Chariot	Leave confinement behind. Burst the old framework. Overcome what is holding you prisoner (The Tower) and risk a new start (The Chariot).
17/8	The Star/ Adjustment	Consider the matter from a higher standpoint. Become aware of favorable prospects and the range of your plans (The Star). Make a smart decision because the responsibility for the further course of things is in your hands alone (Adjustment).
18/9	The Moon/ The Hermit	Take the path of fear cautiously but decisively. Look for the glimmer of hope on the horizon (The Moon). In the process, don't be influenced or irritated by anyone. Instead, remain true to yourself (The Hermit).
19/10/1	The Sun/ Fortune/ The Magus	Take a lighthearted and optimistic approach to the matter (The Sun). Now is the time to dedicate yourself to this topic (Fortune). You have the power and skill to master the task (The Magus).
20/2	The Aeon/The High Priestess	Place your hopes on a new and an expansive future (The Aeon). At the same time, trust in your inner voice, which is certain to guide you (The High Priestess).
21/3	The Universe/ The Empress	Recognize that you are at home here. Assume your place in this world (The Universe). You will see the lively way in which everything will develop and how the matter grows and thrives (The Empress).
22/4	The Fool*/ The Emperor	The situation must first become really chaotic (The Fool) before a new structure can be formed (The Emperor).

*As the 22nd card of the major arcana, The Fool represents this quintessence, even if it has the number 0.

Methods of Laying Out the Cards

Simple Card Layouts

The simplest way to lay cards is to draw a card for a topic. However, in view of the wide spectrum of possible interpretations, its message may sometimes be unsatisfactory in terms of clarity and meaning. If we draw two cards, one of which illustrates the positive possibilities and the other the problematic aspects, we can often get a much more precise picture by comparing them. We offer helpful card-interpreting texts for this purpose.

Pro and Con

If you are looking for a quick message from the cards, simply draw two cards. The first will show the related possibilities and opportunities, while the second will warn against the associated risks and dangers. To interpret them, use the section called "Encourages" for the first and the section called "Warns Against" for the second. By comparing them, you can see how good the chances are and how high the related risks are, and whether there is more that speaks in favor of or against a plan.

Card for the Day

Drawing a card each morning is a pleasant way to become more familiar with the cards and experience their meaning through everyday occurrences. Their meaning may lie in an apparent experience described in the section "Card for the Day." Or it may also be something small, a subtle phenomenon that we would otherwise easily overlook. When the Card for the Day draws attention to such "trivial matters," then they are significant from the perspective of the unconscious mind. It can be highly enriching to pay more attention to these details and perhaps even experience how they begin to intertwine with each other and grow into something meaningful. Even if it is understandable that the card-interpreting suggestions in this book cannot describe the more subtle levels of the Card for the Day, they may stimulate new insights for discovering such concealed meanings.

Card for the Year

In addition to their interpretation as Cards for the Day, the 22 major arcana are also interpreted on another level—as Cards for the Year. There are various possibilities for determining these cards. They can be calculated by using the cross sum from a person's date of birth, month of birth, and the current year. For example, if you are born on February 1st, the sum for the year 2002 would be 2 + 1 + 2 + 0 + 0 + 2 = 7. (If you were born on December 15, 2002, your number would be 12 + 15 + 2 + 0 + 0 + 2 = 31. Since this result is larger than 22, we once again add the cross sum and get 3 + 1 = 4.) Card 7 of the major arcana, The Chariot, is the Card for the Year from February 1, 2002 to January 31, 2003 for everyone who has a birthday on February 1st. And Card 4, The Emperor, would be the card for the year for the person looking at December 15, 2002.

However, since the tarot is a coincidental oracle, it would actually be more in keeping with its nature to simply draw the Card for the Year instead of calculating it. This can be done on New Year's Eve for the coming calendar year, or on your birthday for the next personal year. In any case, always draw this card from the 22 cards of the major arcana. Do this by sorting them out of the pile of cards since only these 22 cards have the depth of meaning that does justice to the yearly theme.

COMPREHENSIVE
LAYOUTS

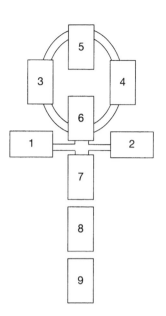

THE ANKH

Statement	Causes, background, and prospects.
Degree of difficulty	4
Cards to draw	9
Typical question	What is the reason for my crisis (illness, problem, etc.) and what prospects do I have?
Special characteristics	The best card-laying method for exploring the background of a situation.

This system of card-laying is based on an ancient Egyptian symbol, the ankh, which is also called the tau cross. It consists of a circle and a cross. In accordance with the meaning of the circle, the cards laid in this area give an answer regarding the emotional background and the deeper-rooted causes, while the cards on the level of the cross show how the problem is expressed on the level of reality, what concrete steps can be taken, and with what prospects we can reckon.

THE MEANING OF THE VARIOUS CARD POSITIONS

1 + 2 = Represent two current impulses, energies, or attitudes that block
each other. You are being crucified between them.[1]
3 = Early causes
4 = Triggering causes
5 = Higher perception
6 = Necessary conclusions

Under the assumption that the perception (5) has taken place and the conclusions
(6) have been drawn, the following shows the further progression:

7 = The next step
8 = Surprising experiences
9 = The result

HOW TO READ THE SPREAD

First find the nature of the conflict or contradiction that exists between Cards 1
and 2. This is the greatest difficulty in this particular spread. Above all, when both
cards depict themes that tend to be pleasant, it isn't easy to see where the problem
lies. However, without this perception, the entire reading will be unsatisfactory.
Then interpret Positions 3 and 4, of which the former can often only be comprehended in a vague manner. The emphasis of the reading should be on Cards 5 and
6 because only the steps related to them involve a possible solution. Use the key
words in the section "Consciousness" for Position 5 and the text under "Encourages" for Position 6. Then look at the future-oriented cards in Positions 7 to 9.

---

[1] This naturally applies only when this card-laying method is used to question the cause of a crisis.
If, on the other hand, we ask about the background of a pleasant experience, these two cards show
what elements harmoniously complement each other.

THE ASTROLOGICAL
TAROT READING

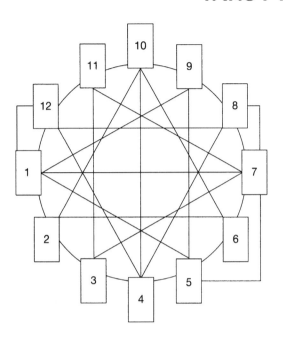

Statement	Extensive description of the present and out-look on future tendencies.
Degree of difficulty	4
Cards to draw	12
Typical questions	Where am I in my life right now? What will my essential experiences be or what will occur during the next month or in the year X? (Without time limitations, the cards reflect the present and immediate future.)
Special characteristics	The card-laying method that includes all areas of life.

Unlike most other card-laying systems, the Astrological Tarot Reading uses the 12-house concept of astrology and makes it possible to ask extensive questions of the tarot. It gives us insight into the 12 areas of life (or astrological houses). In this respect, this card-laying system is a good start for an extensive consultation. The areas emphasized by the important cards can subsequently be explored more deeply by laying the cards again.

THE MEANING OF THE INDIVIDUAL POSITIONS

1 = Basic mood: Significant for the way in which experiences of all the other fields are regarded.

2 = Finances: Security. Dealing with money. Income and expenditures.

3 = Everyday experiences: Themes that affect the area that takes up the most time in our lives.

4 = The home: The area in which we feel protected, in which we know we are rooted. The sense of security that we long for when the outside world becomes too threatening.

5 = Everything that is fun: Games and pleasures of all kinds. Games with children, games with money. The game of love (only becomes serious in Position 7), hobbies.

6 = Work: The current task, the type of work, working methods, the everyday work life.

7 = Partnership: The relationship, marriage, lasting love relationships.

8 = The hidden aspects: All taboos and their transgressions. Particularly sexuality, as well as esoteric experiences. If this interpretation is too inaccessible or intimate for you, you can also call the meaning of this field "Crises and Overcoming Them."

9 = Higher perceptions: Expansion of our own horizons through inner and outer journeys. Convictions, perceptions, and firmly held beliefs, as well as the resulting principles and "good resolutions."

10 = Public recognition: Especially professional success and the future of an occupation.

11 = Friends: Friendships, ideals of friendship, group experiences, and hospitality.

12 = Secret hopes and fears: Longings and misgivings that are related to one or more of the other fields of the circle.

How to Read the Spread

In order to attain an overall message, first interpret the individual cards in their respective positions. During this first attempt, some statements will often be very vague and hazy. Then explore the following positions to see if there are possible connections, which will then result in a more meaningful interpretation:

The Main Axes

Position 1 and 7	= The I/you themes
Position 4 and 10	= From where and to where

The house elements (also called triads)

Positions 1, 5, and 9	= The fire triad, which frequently says something about temperament and self-development.
Positions 2, 6, and 10	= The earth triad, which corresponds to the world of money and work.
Positions 3, 7, and 11	= The air triad, which reflects the level of thoughts, ideas, contacts, and conversations.
Position 4, 8, and 12	= The water triad, which represents feelings and intuitive understanding, yearnings, and moods.

The first look at all the cards doesn't necessarily have to lead to a common overall statement. It may well be that no comprehensible correlation can be found between the individual cards. If this is so, go on to the next step:

Other Connections

In terms of the theme, a connection can frequently be recognized between Positions 5 (flirts, affairs, and casual relationships), 7 (relationships, marriage), and 8 (sexuality). The hopes and fears in Position 12 can often be explained through the basic mood in Position 1.

In conclusion, connect all the individual statements into an overall picture and then determine the quintessence.

THE RELATIONSHIP GAME

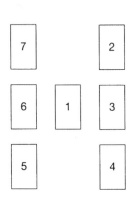

Statement	Status of relationship between two people.
Degree of difficulty	2
Cards to draw	7
Typical questions	What is the nature of my relationship to X?
Special characteristics	The best card-laying method for finding out how two people relate to each other.

This card-laying method is usually used for asking about the status of a love relationship. However, it can also be used for any professional, family, or other relationship. The left column (7,6,5) represents the asker, the right column (2,3,4) stands for the partner or partners.

THE MEANING OF THE VARIOUS CARD POSITIONS

1 = The significator shows the situation that the relationship is in; the theme that rules the relationship.

7 + 2 = These two cards show the conscious level upon which the partners encounter each other. It shows what each person thinks and how they each consciously assess the relationship.

6 + 3 = The middle two cards represent the emotional realm of the relationship and show what each of them holds, feels, senses, longs for, or fears.

5 + 4 = The lower cards signify appearance and behavior, the attitude shown to the outside world. This is possibly a facade that is displayed, independent of the thoughts (upper level) and feelings (middle level) behind it.

HOW TO READ THE SPREAD

From Position 1, first read the theme that currently rules the relationship. Then interpret the individual columns, meaning how both people relate to each other on the respective levels. In conclusion, try to evaluate the dynamic of the relationship: do both people reach out to each other? Or does only one do so? Are both waiting for the other to take the first step?

SPECIAL CHARACTERISTICS

Since the Court cards can depict individuals, these cards naturally take on a special role in The Relationship Game. A card personifying a person of the same sex usually embodies the self-image of the respective person in the area where the card appears. On the other hand, when a Queen or Princess appears on the man's side, or a Knight or Prince on the woman's side, these cards of the opposite sex can have two different meanings. They either show that the respective individual is thinking of such a person (Cards 7 or 2), holds this person in his or her heart (Cards 6 or 3), and/or is involved in a relationship with this person (Cards 5 or 4), or it illustrates an ideal image that this person holds.

THE BLIND SPOT

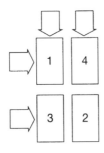

Statement	Self-knowledge.
Degree of difficulty	3
Cards to draw	4
Typical questions	Where am I in my life? Who am I?
Special characteristics	The simplest among the generally difficult card-laying methods related to self-knowledge.

This card-laying method has been derived from the model known as the Johari Window[2] in psychology. It shows four aspects of the personality and gives information about how we perceive ourselves in contrast to the way others see us.

The Meaning of the Various Card Positions

1 = Clear-cut identity: In the thematic area of this card we perceive ourselves in the same manner as others see us.

2 = The great unknown: Unconscious processes and unconscious driving forces that are very powerful, although we ourselves and others are not aware of them.

---

[2]Joseph Luft, *Group Processes: An Introduction to Group Dynamics* (Palo Alto, CA: Mayfield Publishing, 1970), pp. 11–20.

3 = The shadow, what is concealed: Aspects of our being that are known to us, yet we hide—for whatever reasons—from the eyes of others.

4 = The blind spot: Manners of behavior that others perceive in us, but of which—at least to this degree—we ourselves are not aware.

How to Read this Spread

Begin with the card in Position 1, which is the easiest to understand. Then try to find out the nature of the "unknown," which is illustrated by the card in Position 2. Perceiving this aspect is usually the most valuable part of this card-laying system, since unconscious forces are highly active. However, we usually experience them just passively or from the perspective of suffering as long as we are unaware of them. If this is a difficult theme, becoming conscious of it is an advantage, since it makes it possible for us to deal with this predisposition in a more thoughtful, sensible, and perhaps even a more positive way. If this is a valuable characteristic, then becoming conscious of it is naturally an enriching experience.

The two remaining cards have an additional secondary meaning: Position 3 also reflects self-appraisal and Position 4 shows how others see us. If these two statements deviate greatly from each other, if our self-appraisal is considerably different from how others see us, this should be understood as a warning. If others appraise us totally differently than we do ourselves, it could very well be that we have a false image of ourselves.

When the cards are laid for the purpose of self-knowledge, they often are not understood at first glance. This is why it is advisable to leave the drawn cards in their positions for a while and look at them repeatedly. Particularly when we don't give them our undivided attention or stare at them, the pictures can awaken associations within us that suddenly make us aware of their message.

THE DECISION GAME

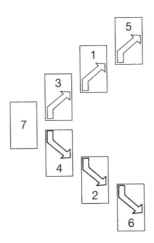

Statement	Two possible tendencies, help in decision-making.
Degree of difficulty	2
Cards to draw	7
Typical questions	How should I decide? What will happen if I do X, and what will happen if I don't do X?
Special characteristics	This card-laying method makes it clear that the asker always has a number of possibilities and is not bound to one exclusive tendency.

Tarot cannot take any decisions out of our hands. It can only illuminate the range of themes associated with the question. In this respect, The Decision Game presented here is not suitable for questions that can be answered with either "yes" or "no." Instead, it shows two possible paths and leaves it up to the asker to choose between the two. More than the others, this card-laying method lets us clearly perceive that the tarot doesn't bind us to one tendency. On the contrary, the asker designs his or her own future by choosing which path to take.

The Meaning of the Various Card Positions

> 7 = The significator. It presents a vivid portrayal of the question's background, the problem, or how the asker sees the decision.
>
> 3, 1, 5 = In this order, these cards show chronologically what will happen if you do X.
>
> 4, 2, 6 = In this order, these cards show chronologically what will happen if you do not do X.

How to Read the Spread

Don't let yourself be irritated by the peculiar order in which the cards are turned over. The reason for this lies in the creation of this card-laying method, but it has no influence on the way in which the cards are read. Begin with Position 7, which can show you what the question is about, what has led to the question, what should be taken into consideration in the decision, or how the decision should be made. Then interpret each of the upper cards from left to right (3, 1, and 5), followed by the lower cards (4, 2, and 6). In conclusion, carefully consider which of the two paths is more advantageous. Remember that each first card (3 and 4) respectively shows how the development begins, the next card (1 and 2) shows how it continues, and the last card (5 and 6) shows where the development is headed. This is why Cards 5 and 6 are the most important: They represent the long-term prospects.

Special Characteristics

In this card-laying method, there are so-called signal cards that show which alternative the tarot favors. If one of the following cards is found on one of the two paths, this means a clear recommendation for taking this direction. If these cards appear on both paths, then consider whether both paths can be taken at the same time or at least one after the other. These cards have no special meaning in Position 7.

1. The Lovers (VI) means that the decision has probably already been made in favor of the path on which this card appears.

2. The Fortune (X) card shows that the asker is not free to choose but, at least at the beginning, must take the path on which this card appears.

3. The Star (XVII) shows the path of the future.

4. Aeon (XX) also shows the path of the future.

5. The Universe (XXI) stands for the proper, true place where the asker belongs.

THE SECRET OF THE HIGH PRIESTESS

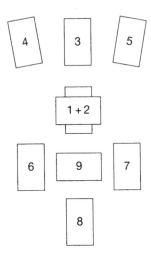

Statement	Course of a matter and its concealed background.
Degree of difficulty	3
Cards to draw	9
Typical questions	How will my plans develop? How will things continue (in my work, etc.)?
Special characteristics	A possible answer that reveals the meaning of the situation.

This card-laying method has been "borrowed" from the Waite Tarot. It has been created on the basis of The High Priestess, as shown in that deck. The fascinating thing about this method is that it not only indicates the trend to be expected, but also possibly reveals a secret: The answer to the enigmatic question of "why?" The three-times threefold Moon Goddess speaks through the nine cards. They are laid out in keeping with the main symbols that surround her:

The Meaning of the Various Card Positions

1 + 2 = The cross on her chest shows the topic in question in the form of two main impulses that can strengthen or hinder each other.

Cards 4, 3, and 5 correspond to the three Moon phases of her crown and show the influential forces effecting the theme:

3 = The Full Moon represents the current main influence.
4 = The Waxing Moon is the power that is gaining influence.
5 = The Waning Moon shows the power that is losing influence.

The two columns at her side represent:

6 = What is in the dark. This means what is there but cannot (yet) be consciously perceived, although it may already be sensed or feared. An unconscious driving force.
7 = What is in the light. This means what is clearly recognized and usually also valued.

The Moon barque at her feet shows:

8 = Where the journey leads, what will come next.

The ninth card, the book of secret knowledge on her lap, is initially concealed as it is laid. Only when all of the other cards have been read may this card be examined. If it is one of the major arcana, the High Priestess has revealed her secret and the card is turned faceup. She has then told us something about the deeper motivations behind the theme in question, the reason and purpose of the development. If it is one of the cards of the minor arcana, it remains concealed. In this case, the High Priestess has kept the secret for herself. The ninth card then has no significance and is not included when calculating the quintessence.

How to Read the Spread

Start with the two main impulses in Positions 1 and 2. Then evaluate the extent to which these complement, strengthen, hinder, or block each other. In this process, Position 1 always shows the first impulse while the additional theme results from Position 2. Then interpret the influences chronologically in the order of 5, 3, and 4. Afterward, evaluate the conscious attitude or expectation (7) before you interpret the unconscious aspect (6). Remember that this concerns an inner driving force that often has a much stronger effect than the conscious attitude (7). Then interpret the prospect card (8) and summarize the future perspectives that result from Cards 4 (future influences), 6 (still unconscious, later possibly becoming conscious), and 8 (further prospects). Only now should you turn over the ninth card and try to comprehend its deeper meaning if it is one of the major arcana.

THE CELTIC CROSS

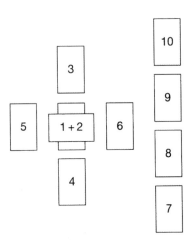

Statement	All-purpose card-laying method, especially for trend developments.
Degree of difficulty	2
Cards to draw	10
Typical questions	How will my plans develop?
Special characteristics	How will things progress? What is happening in my professional life?

This card-laying system is suited for any question. The Celtic Cross is the best-known spread and has been passed down from earlier ages. It is an all-purpose system of laying the cards, which can be used for all forms of questions, but especially for trend development, for illuminating the background of something, as foresight, or for researching the cause. If you are not sure which spread is best suited for asking a certain question, you can always use the Celtic Cross.

Here is an old card-laying saying for it:

- 1 = This is it.
- 2 = This crosses it.
- 3 = This crowns it.
- 4 = It rests upon this.
- 5 = This was before.
- 6 = This comes afterward.
- 7 = This is the asker.
- 8 = This is where it takes place.
- 9 = These are the hopes and fears.
- 10 = This is where it leads.

Here is the less magical approach:

- 1 = This is what is deals with.
- 2 = This is added to it.
- 3 = This is recognized.
- 4 = This is sensed.
- 5 = This has led there.
- 6 = This is how it continues.
- 7 = This is how the asker sees it.
- 8 = This is how the others see it, or where it takes place.
- 9 = This is what the asker expects or fears.
- 10 = This is where it leads.

THE MEANING OF THE VARIOUS CARD POSITIONS

- 1 = The initial situation.
- 2 = The additional impulse, which can be beneficial or hindering.

In these two cards we have the basic answer as to what is. The next two cards give us background information:

- 3 = The conscious level. That which is clear to the asker in dealing with the topic, what is recognized, what is seen, and possibly also what is consciously aimed at.
- 4 = The realm of the unconscious. "It rests upon this" is the magical formula. It thereby expresses that a matter is well anchored on this level and carried by a deep inner certainty with the sturdiest of roots and little tendency toward becoming unsettled.

There is a certain interpretive latitude for the meaning of these cards. Ultimately, however, they reflect what the head (3) and the heart (4) have to say.

5 = The card leading back in time. It shows the most recent past and thereby frequently also gives an indication about the causes of the current situation.

6 = The first card indicating the future gives us a glimpse into the near future and what is to come next.

7 = This card shows the asker[3] his or her attitude toward the topic (Cards 1 and 2) or how the asker feels in relation to it.

8 = The surrounding environment. This can be the location of the event, as well as the influence of other people upon the topic represented. If the question refers to a relationship between two people, this card will basically represent the partner.

9 = Hopes and fears. The significance of this card is frequently underestimated because it has no prognostic character. Yet, it can give us valuable information, especially when we read the cards for someone else. It shows how the asker evaluates the situation, including the related hopes and fears.

10 = The second card indicating the future gives the long-term outlook and the culmination of the development.

The prognostic cards are found exclusively in Positions 6 and 10. All other cards give important additional and explanatory information about the surrounding environment and the background of the topic in question.

HOW TO READ THE SPREAD

Start with Position 5 (past, history) and then read Position 9 (hopes and fears). This will help you have a better idea because you now know the background of the occurrences (Position 5) for the question asked and what the asker expects (Position 9). Next, interpret Cards 1 and 2 as the current main impulse, whereby Card 1 is always the first impulse and Card 2 shows the additional theme that complements, hinders, or promotes it.

Observe what is consciously seen (Position 3) in the process and how it is anchored in the unconscious (Position 4). This position is particularly important. Whatever is rooted here will also weather the worst storms. But if there is a difficult card with problematic roots here, this will have an adverse effect, even if the rest of the cards have a favorable message. Then examine the attitude of the asker toward the topic (Position 7), the external influences or the surrounding environment (Position 8) before you conclude with the prognostic cards in Positions 6 and 10.

---

[3]When the cards are questioned for a person who is not present, you must first be clear about whether this position should reflect your own attitude or that of the other person concerned.

THE CROSS

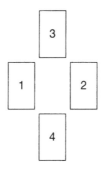

Statement	Evaluating a situation, suggestion and trend development.
Degree of difficulty	1
Cards to draw	4
Typical questions	What is the status of my work, my relationship, or my plans? How should I behave?
Special characteristics	The simplest way of letting the cards evaluate something.

The Cross is one of the most simple, yet interesting of all the card-laying systems. It gives a short, succinct statement that frequently indicates a valuable direction. At the same time, it can be used in very versatile ways. If you are still largely unfamiliar with the 78 tarot cards and their number is confusing to you, you can use this spread by limiting yourself to just the 22 cards of the major arcana. The cards are laid as follows:

THE MEANING OF THE VARIOUS CARD POSITIONS

    1 = It deals with this.
    2 = You should not do this.
    3 = You should do this.
    4 = This is where it leads, this is what it is good for.

How to Read the Spread

Start with Card 1, which sometimes triggers a true "aha" experience, but just gives insignificant information to others. Next, it is especially important to work out the difference between Cards 2 and 3 because they express the actual advice of the cards. For similar cards, it is precisely the subtle difference that can contain the essential points of the message. In conclusion, read the card in Position 4 to find out where the development is heading (in the near future).

Variations

You can use the same card-laying system if you do not understand a card you have read. You should then mix all the cards again and lay them according to this method with the question: What is the meaning of card X as it was laid last time? *In this case, the positions have the following meaning:*

1 = It deals with this.
2 = The card does not mean this.
3 = It means this.
4 = It serves this purpose, this is what it is good for.

THE NEXT STEP

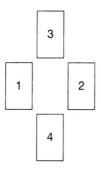

Statement	Suggestion as to what should be done next.
Degree of difficulty	1
Cards to draw	4
Typical questions	What is my next step?
Special characteristics	The card-laying method for frequently asking questions of the cards. Ideal for letting the tarot lead you to a goal you have set.

Whenever you would like to let the tarot guide you to a goal or if you are looking for a guide to lead you around tricky corners, choose this card-laying method. It doesn't show where the path ultimately leads,[4] but what you should do next. Since the message of the cards is always related to a brief period of time, usually no more than 14 days, this approach is most suited for themes where you want to lay the cards more frequently to get new ideas time and again. In addition, the tarot may also tell you when you should lay the cards again.

---

[4]If you would like to find this out, then you should lay The Celtic Cross, The Secret of The High Priestess, or The Path.

THE MEANING OF THE VARIOUS CARD POSITIONS

> 1 = The initial situation; where the asker stands right now.
> 2 = This isn't important yet. This doesn't need to be feared or hoped for at the moment.
> 3 = Only this is important.
> 4 = This is where the next step leads. As soon as this experience occurs, it is time to lay the cards again.

HOW TO READ THE SPREAD

Cards 1 and 4 show the beginning and end of the next step. However, excessive importance should not be given to Card 4. It primarily tells you when the cards should be laid the next time, meaning when the step described here has been completed. This is the moment in which the experience shown by Position 4 has been had, even if it just lasts for a few minutes. The most important card is found in Position 3. It shows what should be observed during the entire time frame—what will truly help you progress. In a certain sense, Card 2 is a warning, since any energy flowing in this direction is wasted. The experience shown here is quite certain not to occur during *this* step.

THE FOOL'S GAME

| 1 | 2 | 3 | 4 | 5 | 6 | 7 | 8 | 9 | 10 | 11 | 12 | 13 |

Statement	Current position and perspectives within a longer development.
Degree of difficulty	4
Cards to draw	12
Typical questions	Where am I in my career? How far have I progressed on my path (of self-realization, spiritual search, psychoanalysis, etc.)?
Special characteristics	The layout to use for contemplating developments over a long period of time.

In a simple progression of cards, The Fool's Game reflects the chronological course of a matter. At the same time, it shows where the asker currently stands within this development, what the asker has already experienced, and what still lies ahead. This is why this spread is more suitable than any other for the observation of far-reaching developments. Because the individual positions have no given interpretation of their own, and every card builds solely upon the previous one, it is in some cases difficult to read these cards. A further complicating factor is that each card indicates a different time frame than another card. It illustrates the order of the experiences, but not the time required for the individual steps. The main difficulty in interpretation, however, lies in the frequently encountered obsession that the development of our lives must somehow take a logical course. In contrast, The Fool's Game frequently shows our contradictions, regressions, new beginnings, and all our false paths and detours.

Lay the cards as follows:

First take The Fool out of the deck. Then shuffle and spread the remaining 77 cards like a fan. The asker then draws 12 of the cards, and mixes The Fool in with them. After the asker has decided whether to uncover the cards "from above" or "from below,"[5] all 13 cards are spread out next to each other.

THE MEANING OF THE VARIOUS CARD POSITIONS

The Fool characterizes the respective point of the present. All the cards that lie behind him (to the left) show past developments, and the cards ahead of him indicate the future. If The Fool comes up as the first card, this means that the asker is still at the beginning of a development or is making a new start. As the last card, The Fool shows that the asker is at the end of this development or at least at the end of an important period of experience.

HOW TO READ THE SPREAD

First look at the cards to the left of The Fool, for these are the past experiences. Then read the cards about the future. Don't let yourself be irritated by relapses or apparent contradictions. Also, don't make the mistake of wanting to attribute the same period of time to each card. Instead, take into consideration that cards following each other may also belong together and may be experienced at the same time.

---

[5]This means whether you start with the top or the bottom card when laying the cards.

THE PARTNER GAME

```
┌─────┐   ┌─────┐
│     │   │     │
│ 1 A │   │ 1 B │
│     │   │     │
└─────┘   └─────┘

┌─────┐   ┌─────┐
│     │   │     │
│ 2 A │   │ 2 B │
│     │   │     │
└─────┘   └─────┘

┌─────┐   ┌─────┐
│     │   │     │
│ 3 A │   │ 3 B │
│     │   │     │
└─────┘   └─────┘
```

Statement	How the partners relate to each other.
Degree of difficulty	1
Cards to draw	6
Typical questions	What is the state of our relationship? How do we feel about each other?
Special characteristics	In this way of laying the cards, the cards are drawn by both partners at the same time.

In addition to its often surprising expressive value, this card-laying method often has the effect of sparking a helpful discussion between partners. Since this spread can be done with just the 22 cards of the major arcana, it is well suited for tarot beginners.

Each of the two partners simultaneously draws three cards in a row and presents them to the other person. When turning over the individual cards, the respective partner says:

1A = This is how I see you.
1B = This is how I see you.
2A = This is how I see me.
2B = This is how I see me.
3A = This is how I see our relationship.
3B = This is how I see our relationship.

HOW TO READ THE SPREAD

One special feature of this card-laying method is determining the quintessence on all three levels. Calculate it once from all the cards as the exhortation to both of the partners; then add it up as advice for each of them individually from the three cards that they have drawn themselves.

THE PLAN GAME

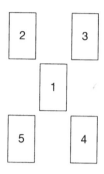

Statement	Suggestions for attaining a goal.
Degree of difficulty	2
Cards to draw	5
Typical questions	How can I attain my goal? How can I achieve more order/satisfaction/money, etc.? How can I win him/her for myself?
Special characteristics	For the two most important positions of this card-laying method, you will find preformulated interpretive text in the card section.

With The Plan Game, a certain plan is illuminated by the cards for they show whether or not (and how) a desired wish can become reality. Draw 5 cards for this purpose.

THE MEANING OF THE VARIOUS CARD POSITIONS

    1 = The significator. A characteristic statement or important thought about this plan.
    2 = The asker's (unconscious) driving force.
    3 = External objections or encouragement.
    4 = This is how it won't succeed.
    5 = This is how it will succeed.

How to Read the Spread

Start with Position 1 in order to recognize the general state of the matter or what information the tarot will give the asker in advance. Position 2 then shows you what motivates the asker; Position 3 is the echo, the support, or the resistance that comes from the outside. You can use the card descriptions found in the interpretive text to read the outcome. Use the "Warns Against" section for Position 4 and "Encourages" for Position 5. Positions 4 and 5 are very decisive positions in this spread.

THE DOOR

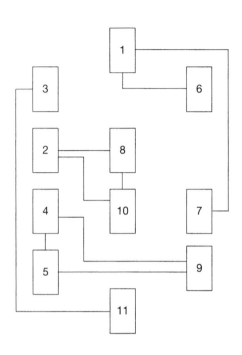

Statement	Pictorial description of a threshold that lies before us.
Degree of difficulty	4
Cards to draw	11
Typical questions	What should I expect to find behind the next door, threshold, challenge, etc.? Should I risk a certain step? What is waiting for me?
Special characteristics	This card-laying method provides a very pictorial answer and is therefore especially well suited for an intuitive interpretation.

This system of laying the cards is particularly good for intuitive card-readers who don't like to be bound by narrow statements of meaning. However, precisely because of the wealth of images involved in this method, it requires a certain amount of practice. This makes it less suitable for beginners.

The Meaning of the Various Card Positions

1 = The name of the door; this is what it is about.
2 = The keyhole; a first idea of what is behind the door.
3 = The lock; this has held the door closed up until now.
4 = The knob; you need it to open the door.
5 = This leads to the door.
6 = Hopes and fears; the asker's expectations regarding what could be behind the door.
7 = The asker's attitude toward the door.
8 = What is actually behind the door.
9 = Where the door can be found.
10 = What happens when the door is opened.
11 = The key to the door, which should fit into the lock (3).

Note: We don't have to go through every door. The cards can also warn us about a trapdoor. Then you should keep the key in a safe place.

How to Read the Spread

The name of the door is just the outer view of it and corresponds with the headlines above a newspaper article. The keyhole (2) provides the details. However, the most important card for what is to come lies in Position 8. It shows where the path through this door will lead in the long run. On the other hand, Position 10 shows more of a short-term feeling or experience in crossing this threshold. First read these positions so you can decide whether it is good to open this door. Positions 6 and 7 reflect the asker's purely subjective expectations. Examine whether these will be justified or disappointed. Compare Position 6 with Position 8 (long-term perspectives) and Position 7 with Position 10 (short-term experiences). Important preconditions for reaching the door are found in Positions 4, 5, and 9—and, last but not least, in Position 11. This opens the lock (Position 3) that has kept the door closed up until now.

THE PATH

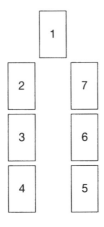

Statement	The best way to achieve a goal.
Degree of difficulty	3
Cards to draw	7
Typical questions	What can I do to achieve X, Y, or Z? How can I find living quarters, a partner for life, a good job, etc.?
Special characteristics	The card-laying method that shows opportunities and perspectives, as well as how to attain them.

The Path shows the possibilities for achieving a desired goal, how the asker has behaved up to this point, and what he or she should do (instead) in the future.

THE MEANING OF THE VARIOUS CARD POSITIONS

　　1 = This is what it's about. This can be achieved.

The left column shows the previous behavior on the following levels:

　　2 = Conscious attitude and rational behavior. What the asker has thought, what has been assumed up until now.

3 = Unconscious attitude, emotional behavior, wishes, desires, hopes, and fears. What the asker feels or has felt up to now.

4 = Outer stance. The effect the asker has on others and the impression made on others. Also possibly his or her facade.

The right column shows suggestions for future behavior, through which this goal can be achieved. The meanings correspond with Positions 2, 3, and 4:

7 = Conscious attitude. Suggest a new way of looking at things.

6 = Emotional stance. Suggest feelings the asker should open up to.

5 = Outer stance. This is how the asker should act, what he or she should do and make known to others.

How to Read the Spread

First, evaluate the prospects shown by the card in Position 1. Does the plan seem promising? Would this path be worth taking? If not, then the desired goal either cannot be attained or perhaps this isn't the right time for this plan. Then the question should be asked again at another time. However, if the goal is worth striving for, consider the individual levels in order to learn where changes are necessary and advisable, as well as to what degree they should be made. For this purpose, compare Cards 2 and 7, 3 and 6, as well as 4 and 5. Special emphasis should be given to the card in Position 6 because it shows in concrete terms what the asker should do.

KEYWORDS
FOR INTERPRETATION

Introduction

If the meaning of each individual tarot card could be reduced to one single concept, the pictures would be superfluous and the cards could just bear one word, such as "Happiness," "Bad Luck," "Fear," "Courage," "Gain," or "Loss." But since a picture is known to say more than a thousand words, the message of each card is more diverse than can be comprehended through its name or a catchword. The key to its meaning is found in the rich symbolism of the card. Since Aleister Crowley studied the esoteric or secret teachings from the East, as well as the esoteric traditions of the West, and was very knowledgeable about a great variety of spiritual schools, it is no wonder that a highly complex symbolism flowed into these cards. Consequently, this deck has a special intensity. In order to make the complex messages understandable, all the card interpretations begin by explaining the symbols.

Yet, it is the nature of symbols to be ambiguous. A circle can symbolize both "zero"—nothing—or something that includes everything. But this doesn't mean that symbols can be interpreted in whatever way we desire. The tarot deck created by Aleister Crowley and Lady Frieda Harris only serves to demonstrate how consistently the message of the cards can be expressed on a great many levels.

Only by translating the symbolism can we understand why the meaning of the Crowley cards clearly deviates from other tarot decks, and why both interpretations can still be correct. When, for example, the number 2 stands for polarity, its spectrum of interpretation ranges from attraction to uniformity to friction, rivalry and enmity. We could also say it ranges from twosomeness to twins to doubt, discord, and dissension. If we combine these two themes with the fire element, which is represented by the Wands in the tarot, various interpretation possibilities are easier to understand. If two burning logs are placed on top of each other, they burn more intensely. If, on the other hand, they are pulled apart, their firepower is weakened, perhaps even extinguished. This is the reason for the contrary messages of the Two of Wands, which are crossed in the Crowley cards and mean "an eagerness to fight," or "strength of will." By way of contrast, they stand parallel to each other in the Waite Tarot and symbolize neutrality, half-heartedness, and indifference.

Since the minor arcana can also be understood using the combined interpretation of number and element, we have added this section to all the number cards in the interpretive section that follows. However, the extensive symbolism of a number, as expressed in the major arcana, should not be sought here. In the minor arcana, the numbers' meaning is lessened; it is an individual aspect from the number spectrum. Table 3 on pages 68–69 shows how numbers are expressed through the minor arcana.

Table 3. Number Symbolism in the Minor Arcana.

NUMBER	MEANING	EMPHASIZED ASPECT	MEANING
1	Activity, initiative, procreative impulse, creative force, yang	Only the impulse that finds a positive echo bears fruit, the others go to waste without having an effect	A good opportunity, a true possibility; however, no guarantee of fulfillment
2	Duality, opposite pole, the other, receptive readiness, passivity, reaction, yin	Varieties of polarity	Unifying, harmonizing, changing, creating rivalry
3	New birth from connection of opposites, liveliness, fertility, synthesis, the divine	Stable basis (a three-legged stool doesn't wobble); fertility	Living development on a stable basis
4	Order, structure, reality, security, earthly	Limitation, solidity, structure	Stability and steadfastness, possibly with a tendency toward rigidity
5	Quintessence, microcosm, meaning, number of humanity, striving for something higher; the number of sin	Crises are part of every form of growth and every higher development	Challenge, crisis
6	Mutual penetration and indissoluble union of opposites, love, equilibrium, harmony, sexuality	Successful union	Success, help, connection
7	Completeness, the divine (3) and earthly (4)	Critical ending and turning point	Exhaustion, crisis, risk

Table 3. Number Symbolism in the Minor Arcana (cont.).

NUMBER	MEANING	EMPHASIZED ASPECT	MEANING
8	Number of the new beginning (7 + 1 = octave), transformation, rebirth (octagonal baptismal font); mediator number between the divine (circle) and earthly (square)	Transformation, renewal	Change, new beginning
9	Turning inward, collecting oneself before stepping into something new	Crystallization	Pleasant or problematic concentration
10	Number of divine order, completeness, sum of the cardinal numbers 1 + 2 + 3 + 4 = 10	Abundance, the whole	Sum, abundance

The astrological classifications of the Crowley cards appear peculiar at times. They are based on the traditions of the Order of the Golden Dawn, to which both Aleister Crowley and Arthur Edward Waite belonged. We have translated the astrological symbols in such a way that the meaning of the card always is visible, even if the same symbols would often be understood in a different way today without the relationship to the respective card. We have accepted Crowley's interpretation of the Hebrew letters associated with the major arcana without any comments.

The interpretation of color also causes some confusion. As enriching as it may be in many cases, there is also a contradictory basis for it, since opposing classifications are found in different cultures. Even within the same tradition, there is a broad range of interpretative possibility. In the West, for example, blue (as the color of the Virgin Mary) represents mercy, humility, chastity, and faithfulness; but it can also represent the intellect, wisdom, and truth. Sometimes it is the depth of the sea, sometimes the cool heights of the heavens. But the dark blue of the sea cannot simply be ascribed to Mary alone because her name means "from the sea," while sky-blue is equated with intellectual flights of fancy. As the Queen of Heaven, heavenly blue can naturally be classified just as easily with the Virgin Mary. Despite this sometimes-confusing complexity of meaning, the color symbolism naturally also opens excellent access to the meaning of the cards.

0 THE FOOL

Symbolism	Meaning
The Fool (April Fool)	Lunacy, lightheartedness
Green clothing	Vital force, freshness
Horns and crystal	High spirits, connectedness of all being
Soles of boots point upward	Weightlessness
Upside-down chalice in the right hand, fire in the left	Union of opposites (chalice = water element)
Grapes	Sweetness of life, intoxication
Rainbow, which surrounds the head	Bridge between Heaven and Earth, conscious ecstasy
Three connected egg- and circle-shaped spirals	Developmental potential on three levels
Spirals with crocodile and tiger	Archaic forces, instinctual nature
Spirals with twin children and blue flower	Naive, cheerful disposition, light-heartedness
Spirals with heart-shaped loop	Highest, sublime level of the heart
Dove of Venus, vulture,[1] butterfly, and winged Sun	Transformative symbols for cycle of life and death
Sun at the root chakra	Creative potency
Coins with astrological symbols	Materialization of archetypal principles
Kabbalah: Aleph א	Ox, plowshare
Astrology: Air element ♎	Lightness, spontaneity

GENERAL: Original potential, creative chaos, carefree, new beginnings, starting off into the unknown, jester's license, foolhardiness

PROFESSION: Starting at zero, playing with various possibilities, creative break, being open for a new beginning, lack of professional experience, chaotic plans, irresponsible

CONSCIOUSNESS: Becoming aware of the almost unlimited abundance of possibilities, brainstorming

PARTNERSHIP: Feelings of Spring, a casual approach, flirting, heartfelt togetherness, new and refreshing encounters, open relationships, experimentation

ENCOURAGES: Try something new in an unbiased and playful manner

WARNS AGAINST: Chaotic circumstances and carelessness

0

AS CARD FOR THE DAY: You should be open to everything today. Be as unbiased as possible. Don't take anything too seriously and even view events that disturb you with playful curiosity. The less you cling to familiar ideas and well-tried pragmatic values, the livelier and more unusual the day will be. In case you discover that you must start at zero again in a certain matter, then be as carefree as possible and risk an unusual beginning. Let yourself be a little crazy today!

AS CARD FOR THE YEAR: In the story of your life, this year may be the meaningful year Zero, in which an important new beginning takes place. Be aware of the many possibilities offered those open for them. Experience the coming twelve months as everlasting springtime. In all due respect, let seriousness and all your worldly wisdom take a year's vacation. Instead, try to encounter life with astonishment, free of biases. Let yourself be guided by curiosity. If you follow intuitive paths without knowing where they lead, you have the opportunity to experience exciting things and can free yourself from normality and apathetic routine. Partake of the Fool's carefree and playful love of life, and it may be that you feel even younger at the end of the year than you do today.

---

[1]Seen only as blue wings.

1 THE MAGUS

The Magus

SYMBOLISM	MEANING
Juggler, balancing on the mountain of the unconscious	Concentration and inspired mental agility
Ankles with a pair of wings	Quickening perceptions
Snake staff, coming from the depths with winged Sun disk above the head	Highest solar mental power, rising from the unconscious mind; consciousness of wholeness
Light-violet triangle	Translucent transcendence
Juggling with the four elements	Lightness, independent approach to reality
Coins	Earth element = deed
Sword	Air element = mind
Fire wand	Fire element = strength of will
Cup	Water element = emotions
Winged egg	Fifth element = quintessence
Scepter with Phoenix head	Power, force that renews itself
Flying arrow	Drive for perception
Parchment	Science
Threatening ape	Intuitive nature, instinctiveness
Kabbalah: Beth ⊐	House
Astrology: Mercury ☿	Skillfulness, cleverness

GENERAL: Primer, activity, resolution, willpower, concentration, vital force, mastery, self-realization, assertion, skillfulness, trickiness

PROFESSION: Taking the initiative, mastering tasks, proving powers of concentration and skillfulness, being successful, passing tests, negotiating in a shrewd and ingenious manner, getting the best of others

CONSCIOUSNESS: Having the highest perceptions, achieving awareness of wholeness

PARTNERSHIP: Fascination, attraction, skillfully mastering problems, taking the first step, accepting oneself and others

ENCOURAGES: Trusting in one's own abilities and proficiently mastering a situation

WARNS AGAINST: Wanting to force something by all means

AS CARD FOR THE DAY: "If not you, then who—and if not now, then when?" is your motto today. Don't hesitate to take the initiative. You have a healthy self-confidence, know what you want, and can skillfully reach your goals with the necessary concentration. You master your tasks easily. Whenever a rock has to be set in motion, wherever you want to prove your abilities, today is the right day to do it. Demonstrate what you can do, stay nimble and coolly independent in discussions and negotiations. Then you will also easily win others for yourself and your cause.

AS CARD FOR THE YEAR: This year promises to be highly successful. Making a true masterpiece of it lies completely in your own hands. You can climb a new peak in a proven area. Explore additional fields of interest and activities that will bring joy and fulfillment in the future. Good opportunities are certain to offer themselves for solving old problems. Don't put your light under a bushel or let someone rob you of your nerve. Instead, show what you can do and take the initiative whenever this move is appropriate. Approach this year actively and prove your sense of enterprise. You now have the necessary skill, the right momentum, and the best cards for realizing your professional and private goals. Whatever you take in hand has good prospects of becoming a genuine hit!

The Priestess

II THE PRIESTESS

SYMBOLISM	MEANING
Veiled female figure	Mystery, concealed knowledge, the unconscious
Bow, curved in the form of fallopian tubes	Fertility, life-giving strength
Bow, which is also a stringed instrument	Artistic strength, bewitchment, temptation
Arrow and bow as a weapon	Protection against undesired intruders
Silver veil with square structure	Archetypal femininity, veiling of the mystery, emotional pattern
Crown of light rays, formed like a crescent and opening upward	Receptivity, key to truth, intuitive knowledge
Seven Moon crescents and Moon crown	Seven planetary spheres that lead to seeing the Highest
Lemniscate (∞) in front of the eyes	Looking at what is eternal
Flowers, fruit, crystals, camel	Fertility, abundance, world of forms, matter
Kabbalah: Gimel ג	Camel
Astrology: Moon ☽	The unconscious, the soul, premonitions, dreams, sixth sense

GENERAL: Inner guidance, wisdom, female intuition, visions, fantasies, secrets, waiting willingness to be guided

PROFESSION: Therapeutic work, artistic and mediumistic abilities, sureness of instinct

CONSCIOUSNESS: Understanding dream messages, having deep spiritual experiences

PARTNERSHIP: Deep affection, emotional connectedness, understanding, mutual trust, letting oneself be found, waiting willingness

ENCOURAGES: Trusting in the inner voice

WARNS AGAINST: Letting oneself drift passively and hoping for a miracle

II

AS CARD FOR THE DAY: Calmly let the present day take its course and watch to see what happens without any intentions or expectations. Let things happen and only intervene when your inner voice tells you to do so. If you can reconcile it with your obligations, you should observe with friendly attentiveness to see what you do when you aren't doing anything. What goes through your mind? What direction do your urges suddenly push you in? Don't force yourself to sit still, but follow your inner impulses. You will be surprised at how intense and fulfilling this apparently idle day becomes. Pay special attention to your dreams, which can give you valuable insights.

AS CARD FOR THE YEAR: A mysterious year lies ahead of you. If you are willing to let yourself be led, you will not only have enriching and unforgettable experiences, but also repeatedly come into contact with hidden forces, the reality behind reality. Trust your intuition. Pay attention to your inner voice, which will guide you at the right time to the places and people who are important for you now. Especially if it is unusual for you to be passively receptive in life instead of actively decisive, you will—after a brief period of adjustment—experience this year of emphasizing free time as highly fulfilling and extremely fascinating. You may want to start keeping a dream journal so you can better understand the messages and advice from your unconscious mind and translate them into your everyday life.

III THE EMPRESS

Symbolism	Meaning
Female figure in pink-green dress with green Moon crown and ruler's cross	Mother Nature, connectedness to Earth, earthly rulership
Zodiac as belt	Ruler of the seasons
The throne's blue columns of flames	Primeval water from which life has come
Posture of body and arms	Alchemical symbol for salt ⊖
Bees on the pink dress	Diligence, fertility, purity
Crescents of the waxing and waning Moon	Life cycle of becoming and dying
Lotus scepter in her right hand	Feminine creativity, life force, beauty that blossoms from the female womb
Opened left hand	Receptiveness, devotion
Sparrow at Empress' back	Latent lustfulness
Alignment and glance at the dove	Peaceableness
Pelican with its young	Motherly love, selflessness
Shield with white double eagle	Lunar, feminine consciousness
Kabbalah: Daleth ד	Door
Astrology: Venus ♀	Sensuality, abundance, enjoyment

GENERAL: Growth, creative potential, intuitive power, renewal, pregnancy, birth, consideration

PROFESSION: Creative work, good opportunities for growth and development, change of occupation, fine antenna for business trends and cycles, hatching new concepts, taking good care of what has been entrusted to one

CONSCIOUSNESS: Insight into the eternal life cycle of becoming and dying

PARTNERSHIP: Lively development, pleasant sensuality, deep trust, addition to the family, sense of security, new and promising perspectives, reviving an old relationship

ENCOURAGES: Trusting in life's forces for growth; being open for changes

WARNS AGAINST: Rampant growth, or letting opportunities slip away without using them

III

AS CARD FOR THE DAY: Look forward to this day. It promises to become very lively. Perhaps you feel drawn out into nature, where mind and soul can recharge. There is a stimulating wind, bringing creative ideas and fertile impulses in your everyday life as well. Something you have been hatching for a long time may come to light today. Something that has stagnated will experience a strong spurt of growth. Whatever you begin anew today has good prospects of developing splendidly, since your distinct antenna for natural processes of development let you instinctively do the right thing.

AS CARD FOR THE YEAR: A fruitful year lies ahead. The coming twelve months will be marked by creative changes and welcome opportunities. Till your field well so you can bring home a rich harvest. This is a good time for promising new beginnings that are focused on expressing more of yourself and your abilities. Open yourself to stimulating, fructifying impulses that let your life become richer and more beautiful. But also something you have been carrying around with you for a long time can now take concrete form and give you a new sense of fulfillment. Trust in the helpful and healing powers of nature.

IV THE EMPEROR

SYMBOLISM	MEANING
Majestic male figure in red- and gold-embroidered clothing	Strength, activity, authority, glory, power
Crossed legs and triangle formed by arms and torso above them	Alchemical sign for sulfur 🜍, masculine energy
Golden bees on the clothing	Diligence, sense of order, royal dignity (attribute of the pharaoh)
Scepter with ram's head	Claim to rulership, power and assertive will, courage
Imperial orb with Maltese cross	Solidified power, law and order as precondition for peace and security
Crown with diamonds	Crystallization of will and power
Rams' heads	Indication of card's association with Aries
Shield with red double eagle	Solar, masculine consciousness
Two Sun disks with stars	Uprightness, continuity
Lamb with flag of victory	Victory of humility
Golden lilies	Attribute of power
Kabbalah: Tzaddi צ	Fishhook
Astrology: Aries ♈	Assertive force, will

GENERAL: Sense of reality, willingness to take responsibility, initiative, sense of security, continuity, strength of leadership, uprightness, pragmatism

PROFESSION: Stability and clear structures, consolidation, realizing plans, working out clear concepts, leadership position, discipline and endurance, perfectionism

CONSCIOUSNESS: Valuing structures of order and uncompromising, realistic thinking

PARTNERSHIP: Clear agreements, secure foundation, well-tested relationship structures, orderly circumstances; realizing mutual goals

ENCOURAGES: Persistently turning intentions and plans into reality

WARNS AGAINST: Stifling everything through exaggerated perfectionism and seriousness

IV

AS CARD FOR THE DAY: You should do a good job in every way today. Whatever there is to be done, whatever you've been wanting to take care of for a long time now, tackle it. Now you have enough energy, the required skill and necessary competence to put things in order, clarify anything that is unclear, and work though unsolved business. If nothing concrete should occur to you, then maybe this just means it's time to thoroughly clean up your living space, fix your bike, or pay old bills.

AS CARD FOR THE YEAR: A year of deeds lies ahead of you. Ideas you have toyed with, wishes you dwell on, intentions you have perhaps often announced will now be put to the acid test. It's time to turn whatever is feasible into action; but throw off any unnecessary ballast. During the coming twelve months, you will display more discipline, endurance, and persistence than you have before. Check to see what goals are particularly important and how you want to make use of this phase. Flexible steadfastness is the magic word for following the red thread until you have turned your plans into reality. The task of the year may naturally also involve making binding decisions, securing what you have achieved, drawing clear boundaries, or assuming more personal responsibility.

The Hierophant

V THE HIEROPHANT

Symbolism	Meaning
High priest	Conviction of faith, wisdom
Masklike facial features	Rigid beliefs, dead rituals
Window with rose petals	Translucent transcendence
Snake above his head	Wisdom, healing
Dove	Holy Spirit, enlightenment
Priest's staff with three rings	Union of past, present, and future
Three pentagrams within each other	Integration of human being into cosmic order
Osiris in large pentagram	Current Age of Osiris[2]
Woman with sword and Moon crescent in middle pentagram	The Age of Isis,[2] which passed about 2000 years ago
Horus child in small pentagram	The beginning Age of Horus[2]
Four cherubim at the four corners	Bearer of the divine altar
Elephant and bull	Perseverance, earthiness
Kabbalah: Vau ו	Nail
Astrology: Taurus ♉	Tradition, steadfastness

[2]In a certain sense, these terms that Crowley coined can be translated as the Era of Matriarchy (Age of Isis), the Age of Pisces (Osiris), and the approaching Age of Aquarius (Horus).

GENERAL: Trust, search for truth, experience of meaning, power of conviction, virtue, expansion of consciousness, strength of faith

PROFESSION: Meaningful activity, following one's calling, high-level work ethic, teaching, higher education, trust in one's own abilities

CONSCIOUSNESS: Having a deep experience of meaning, developing trust in God, expanding one's worldview, self-examination

PARTNERSHIP: Deep trust, confidence, harmony, revelation of love, mature moral ideals, recognizing and appreciating the meaning and value of a relationship

ENCOURAGES: Searching for meaning, doing something worthwhile

WARNS AGAINST: Arrogant self-complacency and a dogmatic know-it-all attitude

V

AS CARD FOR THE DAY: Encounter this day with a healthy trust in God. You have every reason to be confident, as well as good chances of doing or experiencing something truly meaningful. Don't cling to encrusted rituals or listen to hollow phrases and empty promises. Look for what is substantial, for concealed, inner values. Don't let yourself be impressed by external appearances. If you should get involved in a conflict of interests, make your decision in a way that allows you to think back on today with a good conscience.

AS CARD FOR THE YEAR: Meaning is the important factor now. If you have often asked yourself why you do this or that, or what it's all supposed to mean, then you will have the time and opportunity during the coming twelve months to find a convincing answer. In order to do this, you should primarily examine your principles of belief. Whenever you get caught up in empty dogmas or ideals and prejudices, which were perhaps drummed into you as a child, now is the time to replace them with a lively, convincing way of thinking that does justice to your maturity. Whether or not this involves special situations or the meaning of life itself, this year you will have the opportunity to perceive the values that are truly important to you. Don't be surprised if you have come to a new, more spirited philosophy of life at the end of this year.

VI THE LOVERS

SYMBOLISM	MEANING
Black king with gold crown and red lion	Conscious masculine force
White queen with silver crown and white eagle	Conscious feminine force
Black child with club	Inner, unconscious masculinity
White child with bouquet of roses	Inner, unconscious femininity
King and queen give their hands to each other	Union of opposites, love
Black and white child hold hands	Inner opposites also unite
Lance	Conquest, procreative power
Chalice	Devotedness, openness
Cloaked violet figure, who protectively spreads his hands	Holiness, priestly power, divine blessing
Winged egg with snake entwined around it	Secret of life, beginning of the Great Work
Arrow-shooting Cupid	Longing for union
Lilith and Eve	Dark and light aspects of femininity
Dome of swords	Analysis, clear decision
Kabbalah: Zain ז	Sword
Astrology: Gemini ♊	Opposites, exchange

GENERAL: Union, love, heartfelt actions, decisions of the heart, overcoming opposites, collecting details

PROFESSION: Feeling attracted to a task, joining forces with others, ability to make compromises, business fusions, concluding contracts, good teamwork

CONSCIOUSNESS: Recognizing what belongs together

PARTNERSHIP: Lover's bliss, marriage, reconciliation, finding the dream partner, willingness to enter into a relationship, truly opening up to another person, following one's heart, making a clear decision

ENCOURAGES: Joining forces with others and becoming involved in a plan with all one's heart

WARNS AGAINST: Thinking that the beginning is the goal

VI

AS CARD FOR THE DAY: Make a heartfelt decision—which may concern a person, thing, or plan—today. If you have hesitated up to now or were filled with doubts, you should send your rational mind away for the weekend, listen to your inner voice, and have a heart. Examine where you should overcome differences or inner contradictions and put something back together again that has fallen apart or is broken. Drawing this card doesn't always mean that the love of your life is waiting at the next bus stop, but things sometimes actually do happen that way.

AS CARD FOR THE YEAR: This year will thrill your heart. Perhaps the reason is a person you already know or who now comes into your life, or perhaps a fulfilling task or precious experience lets your heart overflow. Whatever it may be, don't approach things in a half-hearted manner but say "yes!" from the depths of your soul. Wherever you have made your happiness dependent upon outer circumstances or other people, you can now recognize that the path to deeper fulfillment begins with overcoming inner resistance and differences. Try to achieve clarity. This will give you the strength to overcome the obstacles at the beginning. You can also eliminate possible misunderstandings, mediate conflicts, and ultimately celebrate the results according to your heart's desire.

VII THE CHARIOT

Symbolism	Meaning
Charioteer with golden armor in meditative position	Focused forces of the soul, inner orientation to the goal
Crab as helmet ornamentation	Indication of this card's association with the sign of Cancer
Grail chalice opening to the front in his hands	Openness, search for fulfillment
Standing red chariot wheels	Present willpower, intention to act, readiness
Blue baldachin supported by four columns	Heavenly tent supported by the columns of Earth
Light, concentric circles in background	Dynamics of eternal, cosmic movement
Center point of Grail chalice in front of the center (solar plexus) of the charioteer and the center of the circles in the background	Harmonizing inner, outer, and cosmic goals into a mutual direction
Four sphinxes with fourfold exchanged body parts in light and dark	Subdivision of the four elements into 16 sub-elements, masculine/feminine
Kabbalah: Cheth ח	Fence
Astrology: Cancer ♋	Taking one's individual path

GENERAL: Mood of departure, thirst for adventure, boldness, conscious of goal, assertive will

PROFESSION: Self-employment, aiming for new projects, ambition, willingness to take a risk, decisiveness, career advancement, taking on new tasks

CONSCIOUSNESS: Inwardly attuning oneself to goal

PARTNERSHIP: New relationship, animating impulse, orientation toward mutual goal, making great leap forward

ENCOURAGES: Tackling the matter immediately, decisively, and purposefully

WARNS AGAINST: Believing that everything has been achieved by just setting out toward the goal

VII

AS CARD FOR THE DAY: Things can finally get underway today. You don't need to wait any longer. Concentrate on your goal and once again check to be sure you have everything you need so that nothing important will be missing, or you suddenly lose energy while underway. However, if you aren't ready to go and haven't even been thinking of setting out, then you should be curious as to what runway will open up today. Something will be certain to get rolling.

AS CARD FOR THE YEAR: Now you can risk the big leap. Open up to adventure. This year stands under the star of a very promising new beginning. At its end, you will be more self-confident and independent. Wherever you want to strive for a major goal, run away from stifling constriction, or overcome personal obstacles, the starting shot will be fired soon. Until the time is ripe for this, once again examine your motivation and the clarity of your envisioned goal. Then take action without hesitation, purposefully and decisively. You have the best chances of achieving what you envision and bringing new energy and a refreshing momentum into your everyday life.

VIII ADJUSTMENT

SYMBOLISM	MEANING
Female figure on tiptoe	Inner equilibrium, highest concentration, balance
Blue-green coloration	Wisdom and contemplation
Mask	Attention focused within
Sword with Moon crescent pommel	Instinctive power of discernment
Balanced scale pans showing Alpha and Omega	Harmony between polarities
Chains upon which the scale pans hang	Connecting links that illustrate the principle of cause and effect
Crown with ostrich feathers	Divine justice
Throne of four pointed pyramids and eight spheres	Limitation, law, equilibrium between round (feminine) and straight (masculine)
Circles with rays in four corners	Balance of light and darkness
Kabbalah: Lamed ל	Out-stretched arm
Astrology: Libra ♎	Balance, objectivity

GENERAL: Objectivity, clarity, balance, justice, karma, sober perception, personal responsibility, self-criticism

PROFESSION: Bearing the consequences, becoming clear about professional goals, good discernment, balanced books, fair contracts, harvesting what one has sown

CONSCIOUSNESS: Recognizing personal responsibility in everything one experiences

PARTNERSHIP: Equal rights, fair agreements, balanced life of a relationship, living together for practical purposes, business relationship

ENCOURAGES: Viewing something objectively and soberly, as well as recognizing one's personal responsibility in it

VIII

WARNS AGAINST: Becoming unable to act because of too much careful consideration

AS CARD FOR THE DAY: It is important to keep a clear head today. If there is a conflict or a decision needs to be made, remain fair and consider the long-term consequences of your actions. It is possible that you will be confronted with the effects of an earlier matter. In keeping with how you behaved at that time, you may now be pleased at the results, or face the day with a queasy feeling in your stomach.

AS CARD FOR THE YEAR: This year is a decisive one. You should take the time to find clarity in important areas and make decisions that are responsible, fair, and balanced in the long run. Otherwise, how you experience the coming twelve months will be completely up to you. Strictly speaking, you are responsible for yourself, since you will harvest what you now sow. This may be very enriching, but it could also be extremely unpleasant, depending on how you have behaved in the past. Should you actually be confronted with disagreeable consequences and unpleasant old burdens, then you can also take advantage of this opportunity. Straighten up what went wrong in the past so that you have peace in the future.

IX THE HERMIT

The Hermit ♍

Symbolism	Meaning
Old man in a bent posture, turning away	Contemplation about oneself, inner collection, concentration on essentials
Red cloak	Courage, strength
White hair	Maturity, wisdom, enlightenment
Glistening diamond with Sun	Light of perception
Tamed Cerebrus, three-headed Hound of Hell	Shadow world integrated into personality
White field	Living nature
World egg with entwined snake	Origin of all things, mystery of Creation
Spermatozoon	Procreative impulse, life potential
Pyramid of rays	Inner vision, spiritual liberation, illumination
Kabbalah: Yod '	Hand
Astrology: Virgo ♍	Preciseness, reliability, asceticism, concentration, harvest

GENERAL: Contemplating what is essential, defining one's position, seclusion, seriousness, retreat, getting to the bottom of things, life experience

PROFESSION: Matured concepts, staking one's hopes on proven goals, recognizing one's true calling, taking one's own path, retreat from professional life, passing on experience to others

CONSCIOUSNESS: Knowing oneself and standing up for oneself

PARTNERSHIP: Taking something seriously, assuming a mature attitude, being true to oneself instead of making lazy compromises, temporary retreat to clarify relationship or conscious choice of single life

ENCOURAGES: Letting something mature, taking oneself seriously

WARNS AGAINST: Embitterment, cranky solitary ways, unworldliness

IX

AS CARD FOR THE DAY: This is your day. Take enough time for yourself and don't get infected by the hectic pace of everyday life. If you must dedicate yourself to a matter, do this with full attentiveness, without being pushed or influenced. In the case of an important decision, let this ripen until you have found your own personal and clear approach to it. Perhaps it will help to meditate, take a long walk, or simply look at a lake until you come to terms with yourself.

AS CARD FOR THE YEAR: Things are getting serious now! And this is meant in the best sense of the word. The year ahead is a time of collection in which it is important to seriously confront yourself and the world to find out what you really want. Use this phase to think about your life. Examine it to see to what extent the contents and outer structures in your professional and private life still correspond to your own nature and individuality. Wherever this is not the case, find out what must change. Such insights are not easy to find, but you do have a whole year to do it. Taking a number of days to retreat into silence—in a monastery, on an island, or some other secluded place—will be very supportive for these perceptions. You should not misunderstand this card and fear that you must spend the year lonely and alone. The Hermit signifies standing up for yourself and being true to yourself, especially during encounters with other people.

X FORTUNE

SYMBOLISM	MEANING
Ten-spoked wheel	Structure, time and space, laws of growth and decay, completion
Heavenly wheel without spokes	Eternity, cosmic clock of fate, perpetual cycle
Yellow stars	Heavenly sign, hope
Lightning bolts	Divine forces that have a fructifying or destructive effect
Violet background	Holiness, divine authority
Three figures on the wheel	Becoming—being—passing
Ape-headed being (Hermanubis) striving upward	Constructive forces, creative spirit, development
Sphinx with sword	Creation, wholeness, existence
Crocodile-headed being (Typhon) striving downward	Annihilating and destructive forces, decay
Ankh and crooked Heka staff	Sign of life and symbol of power
Energy swirls in background	Comprehensive effect of the turning wheel
Kabbalah: Kaph כ	Palm of hand
Astrology: Jupiter ♃	Fortune, abundance, growth

GENERAL: Changes, shift, new beginning, happiness, fateful events, task in life

PROFESSION: Being guided by destiny, finding one's calling

CONSCIOUSNESS: Insight and acceptance of forces larger than the ego

PARTNERSHIP: Happy development in relationship, karmic connections, finding the right partner, fateful encounters, opportunities of understanding one's relationship patterns

ENCOURAGES: Recognizing one's destiny and shaping it as the task in life

WARNS AGAINST: Fatalistic resignation to one's fate

X

AS CARD FOR THE DAY: There are days when we must unavoidably face situations and tasks. If you have the impression today that certain things simply take their course, you shouldn't resist it. You can assume that everything has its appropriateness, even if the meaning is concealed from you at the moment. The chances are good that, at a later date, the whole thing will turn out to be a stroke of luck.

AS CARD FOR THE YEAR: This year will bring you good fortune. The catch is that we don't always immediately understand what is good for us, which is why fate must sometimes force our happiness upon us. How you experience the coming period of time will depend completely on your willingness to open up for the hints of destiny. This concerns a direction that harmonizes with the depths of your individual nature, but not necessarily with what you have thought up for yourself. Which is exactly what can create a dilemma: we suffer because something has turned out differently than we thought it should. Yet, we don't recognize that it is precisely this development that has been lacking for our happiness because it profoundly corresponds with our inner being. The best approach is to explore the time quality of the coming months with the help of astrology, the tarot, or the I Ching to find out in which areas of your life you should open yourself to these changes.

XI LUST

SYMBOLISM	MEANING
Naked, lasciviously enraptured woman with flowing hair	Sexual ecstasy, passion, rapture, divine intoxication, love of life
Seven-headed, lionlike animal	Animalistic drives, instinctual nature, vitality, wildness
Red-glowing fire chalice (uterus) with streaming rays of light and snakes	Sexual energy, vitality, death and rebirth, destruction and renewal
Stars and faces of saints in the violet background	Trampled moral values
The Beast 666	Animal, woman, falling stars, and trampled saints have been taken from the Apocalypse of St. John, which describes the Antichrist as Beast 666 (with which Crowley identified himself) in this manner (see page 10).
Kabbalah: Theth ט	Snake
Astrology: Leo ♌	Joy of life, vitality, courage

92

GENERAL: Courage, vitality, love of life, strength, passion, intrepidity

PROFESSION: Desire to work, commitment, willingness to take risks, creative power, strong motivation, creativity

CONSCIOUSNESS: Encountering the inner animal and taming it with love

PARTNERSHIP: Powerful relationship, passionate connection, fascination, sexual debauchery, excesses

ENCOURAGES: Passionate devotion to a person, a task, an experience

WARNS AGAINST: Just following the pleasure principle and trampling on other people's values

XI

AS CARD FOR THE DAY: Today things may get wild. You feel vital, full of energy, and so brimming with the love of life that you shouldn't be surprised if your passion gets the best of you. This doesn't mean you have to participate in some kind of orgy, but allow yourself a bit of boisterousness in any case. In case you share this desire with another person or translate it into a creative process, you will very much appreciate its prickling and connecting aspect. With your power and strong personal magnetism, you can easily overcome any obstacles and have an attractive and convincing effect on others.

AS CARD FOR THE YEAR: This is a year of passions. It may be that you feel yourself irresistibly drawn to another person, or that you devotedly dedicate yourself to a task or theme. In any case, you can use the life-intensifying and creative energy of this experience to throw overboard oppressive limitations and outdated structures. Don't be surprised if you have a conflict with moral principles that you consider incontestable. In these cases, check to see whether these are true values or just hollow conventionalities from which it would be better to free yourself. If you do so, this year can be pleasurable in the truest sense of the word.

Symbolism	Meaning
Naked figure hanging upside-down	Helplessness, victim attitude, unconditional devotion
Hanging by the left foot	Unconsciously falling into this situation
Crossed legs	Earthly reality
Arms suggest a triangle	Divinity
Cross above triangle	The earthly above the divine, upside-down world, darkening of the light
Faceless, bald head	Identity crisis, loss of ego
Ankh with snake of life	Pole of life, life thread
Radiant, greenish background	Shimmer of hope
Black snake of death beneath the head	Pole of death, facing the unavoidable
Upside-down hanging figure between the snakes	Being crucified between poles that mutually exclude each other
Blue square grid	Narrow pattern of life; compulsive, small-minded thought structures
Green disks	Mercy, redemption
Kabbalah: Mem מ	Water
Astrology: Water element ▽	Devotion, spirituality

GENERAL: Being worn down between two opposites, dilemma, test of patience, powerlessness, dead-end street, involuntary learning processes, crisis in life, forced break, having to make a sacrifice

PROFESSION: Trying tasks, lack of success, drawn-out plans, search for work that appears to be in vain, no perspective for future, being stuck and not knowing how things will continue

CONSCIOUSNESS: Being crucified between contradictions and recognizing the solution in changing one's ways

PARTNERSHIP: Crisis in a relationship, futile efforts, turning in circles, being stuck in a dilemma that can only be overcome by sacrificing something that has been self-evident up until now

ENCOURAGES: Changing one's ways and opening up to new insights

XII

WARNS AGAINST: Resignation, self-sacrifice, or stubbornly insisting upon the same old routine

AS CARD FOR THE DAY: Your patience will be put to a test today. Either something that has already been stuck for a long time will continue to be delayed, or a matter that you didn't expect will suddenly come to a standstill. Don't try to solve the problem with a tour de force. This would only make things worse. Perhaps just changing your perspective would suffice to see the whole thing in a completely different light. If this doesn't help, you will probably have to make a sacrifice one way or the other so that things get moving again.

AS CARD FOR THE YEAR: Let this year become the turning point of your life! You have become stuck in a dead-end street and probably have no choice but to change directions. Even if you have the feeling of being helplessly caught in a trap, you shouldn't let yourself hang in the air, since you will find yourself even deeper in crisis. It doesn't help to violently try to force change. This is like quicksand—the more you struggle, the deeper in you get. If you want things to progress, you will need patience, the willingness to change familiar habits, and must give attention to the problem until the solution becomes clear. This is ultimately quite simple. However, solutions usually tend to seem simple once we finally have found them!

XIII DEATH

SYMBOLISM	MEANING
Black skeleton that cuts the thread of life with a scythe	Transience, end, renunciation
Crown of Osiris, the Egyptian god of death	Death and rebirth
Gateway-shaped posture of leg bones	Gateway to new life
Rising bubbles with light-blue, dancing figures	Ascent to new life
Scorpion	Indicates Scorpio association of this card, symbol of dying and becoming
Wilted lotus and lily blossoms	Transience, formation of humus as precondition for new life
Fish and snake	Death and resurrection
Eagle	Transformation, liberation, overcoming the material world
Kabbalah: Nun נ	Fish
Astrology: Scorpio ♏	Transformation, dying and becoming

GENERAL: Parting, natural end, fear of life, futile clinging, being forced to let go, renunciation

PROFESSION: Finishing a professional activity, fulfilling an assignment, burying occupational goals and projects, retirement

CONSCIOUSNESS: Confronting one's own transience

PARTNERSHIP: End of a relationship, beginning of a fundamental change in the partnership, parting, fear of loss, feelings that have died

ENCOURAGES: Letting go, letting something end

WARNS AGAINST: Steps that have no future

XIII

AS CARD FOR THE DAY: Something is ending today. Something is running out or expiring today. Perhaps you are happy that "it" is finally over. Or perhaps you also have a hard time letting go of something that possibly meant a great deal to you. In any case, you should trust that it is now time to say farewell. Try not to maintain something that has run its course. If you have really freed yourself of it, then you will feel liberated and relieved at the very end, even if it's hard for you to imagine this at the moment.

AS CARD FOR THE YEAR: This year may mean an important turning point in your life. Wherever something has run its course, wherever contents and form are exhausted, this is the time to take leave in order to make room for new developments. So let go wherever you have already been sensing that even the greatest efforts are in vain. Now is the time to finally leave bad or harmful habits behind you and part from anything that no longer does you good. If you are conscious and willing to free yourself from outdated structures, it will be easy and obvious for something new to arise. When the pain and fear of parting with the known are among these experiences, you should acknowledge them without heroically suppressing or downplaying these human feelings.

XIV ART

Symbolism	Meaning
Alchemist as double-headed, androgynous person	Linking masculine and feminine aspects, equilibrium
Many-breasted body	Nurturing forces
Green dress with bees	Naturalness, fertility
Mixture of fire (sulfur) and water (mercury)	Alchemical art of uniting opposites
Golden kettle with skull and raven	Putrefaction and death as necessary fermentation process for new life
White lion and red eagle	The reversal of "normal" reality[3]
Rainbow-colored stream of light with arrow rising from the kettle	Released energy, awakening spirit, perception that shoots upward
Sun arc with the Latin inscription *Visita interiora terrae rectificando invenies occultum lapidem*	The universal solvent: "Visit the interior parts of Earth: by rectification you shall find the hidden stone"
Kabbalah: Samekh ס	Support, foundation
Astrology: Sagittarius ♐	Force that strives for something higher

[3]The lion is normally red and the eagle white, as on the card The Lovers.

GENERAL: Finding the right proportions, balance of powers, harmony, relaxation, overcoming differences, healing

PROFESSION: Resolving conflicts, joyful and productive teamwork, making progress, dissolving contradictions and resistance, finding the balance between work and leisure time

CONSCIOUSNESS: Overcoming inner tensions and finding the way out of an apparently unsolvable dilemma

PARTNERSHIP: True harmony, tantric exchange, deep connectedness, successfully balancing interests, equality in togetherness, "the good mixture"

ENCOURAGES: Giving one's best to overcome contradictions or differences

XIV

WARNS AGAINST: Underestimating the difficulty of a plan or the depths of a problem

AS CARD FOR THE DAY: Today you have a lucky hand with which you can succeed at developing an unusual mixture or a remarkable creation. This could be bringing people together, discovering a clever solution to a problem, or creating an ingenious recipe. Today is practically made for doing things like entering into deep relationships, softening hardened fronts, or reducing tension.

AS CARD FOR THE YEAR: This is the year of the great work, which is what the alchemists called the successful union of opposites. Wherever you find yourself in a tormenting contradiction, feel yourself torn between extremes, or helplessly stuck in a dilemma, whenever the two souls in your breast threaten to tear you apart, during this year you can actually find the solution, the right mixture, that has been impossible up until now. The precondition for this artistic device is the willingness to go deep enough while not clinging to superficialities, apparent self-evident truths, or social conventions. Liberation from an intolerable field of tension is not only one of the happiest moments in life but is also a decisive step in the direction of healing. Make this year into a great work of art.

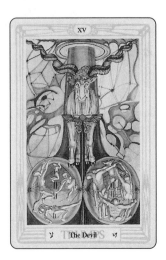

XV THE DEVIL

Symbolism	Meaning
Smiling goat with spiral-formed horns and "third eye"	Pan, the god of nature, procreator of everything, instinctual and sexual nature
Lotus garland	Shows its bearer to be a child of good
Transparent testicles with sperm in the form of human beings	Life-creating forces rest in the depths and mature with time
Phallus-like tree trunk that thrusts into a blue ring, the womb of the Queen of Heaven	Sap of life that rises from the depths
Staff rising from the depths with winged Sun disk (found in the highest position on The Magus)	Light as a child of the darkness
Gray material resembling a spider's web	Snares of the underworld, insidious-ness, danger of entanglement
Kabbalah: Ayin ע	Eye
Astrology: Capricorn ♑	Sign of the greatest darkness of the year, when the Sun is reborn at the Winter Solstice

GENERAL: Shadows, instinctiveness, lack of moderation, greed, thirst for power, temptation, unconscious forces

PROFESSION: Prohibited activities, corruption, exploitation, intrigues, shady dealings, exploitation of dependencies, dark business deals

CONSCIOUSNESS: Encountering one's shadow

PARTNERSHIP: Deep passion, lover's pact, community of fate, emotional entanglements, love spell, fascination, lustfulness, power struggles, hatred, bondage, projections

ENCOURAGES: Bringing light into the darkness

WARNS AGAINST: Destructiveness of natural drives that have been suppressed

XV

AS CARD FOR THE DAY: Even without tempting fate, today you could encounter your dark side. Perhaps you let yourself be seduced into taking a rash step or become tempted to act against your convictions. Or tendencies—such as envy, jealousy, greed, or a thirst for power—are awakened within you that you knew nothing of or that you thought you had long overcome. Becoming annoyed about this or putting the blame on others helps just as little as trying to get a grip on yourself. Use the opportunity to bring light into the darkness by becoming aware of your own unloved aspects and exploring reasons for their existence.

AS CARD FOR THE YEAR: You should clean out your "cellar" this year. In the process, some things will come to light that you knew nothing about. Other things, of which you only had a dark suspicion, suddenly become clear. The cellar naturally means the dark side of human nature that lets us do things over and over—and later we say, "The Devil made us do it." The coming twelve months will offer opportunities to become better acquainted with this aspect. Stop hunting for the scapegoats and ask yourself why you have gotten into these devilish situations. Become aware of how easy you are to seduce. Get to know the split-off and unloved aspects of your inner nature that, as long as they are suppressed, become the inner allies of outer forces, causing you to be weak. Give these shadow beings an appropriate place within you. Find out where and how you can live out these tendencies in the future in a way that is sensible and tolerable.

XVI THE TOWER

SYMBOLISM	MEANING
Stone tower with grated doors and windows	Hardened personality, encrusted consciousness, rigid security-oriented attitude, prison
Fire-spitting maw of the underworld	Upheaval coming from the depths
Collapsing walls	Bursting structures, intense change
Falling square figures	Bold, perhaps even daredevil release of souls that have been hardened by imprisonment
Shining Eye of Shiva	Power of destruction
Dove with twig	Salvation, new hope
Snake-lion Abraxas	Union of light and shadow, talisman
Black background	Destruction, chaos, disaster, darkness
Kabbalah: Pe פ	Mouth
Astrology: Mars ♂	Combative, destructive, rousing force

GENERAL: Sudden perception, upheaval, breakthrough, liberation, blow of fate

PROFESSION: Termination, bankruptcy, radical chance, tour de force

CONSCIOUSNESS: Recognizing fixed ideas and exploding old concepts that have become too constrictive

PARTNERSHIP: Sudden separation, emotional outbursts, breaking out of restrictive relationships, cleansing "storm"

ENCOURAGES: Going beyond a framework that is too narrow

WARNS AGAINST: The incalculable risks and dangers that a radical upheaval brings with it

XVI

AS CARD FOR THE DAY: Things certainly won't be boring today. You should reckon with a surprise that you either welcome as an "aha" experience or see as a vehement disturbance that thwarts your set expectation. Even if it understandably annoys or hurts you when something doesn't go according to plan today, remember that this card ultimately means breaking out of an environment that is too constrictive or being liberated from a fixed idea. In retrospect, you won't mourn long for whatever may possibly fall by the wayside today.

AS CARD FOR THE YEAR: The year ahead may be the year of your liberation, if you have the necessary courage. This is why you should drop the bombshell and burst the framework that has become too small for you. Risk breaking out of constrictive concepts, structures, and lifestyles that keep you imprisoned. Whenever you resist change, run after set ideas, or cling to old habits, it may be necessary to rethink things. You should examine what you may see too one-sidedly or too narrowly. Do you cling to superficial security? If you notice areas of conflict, it's better to let go, because the more you fight for things, the more external circumstances may force you to give them up. These changes are not senseless blows of fate but necessary for your further growth.

XVII THE STAR

SYMBOLISM	MEANING
Naked, blue female figure	Nut, the ruler of the stars
Long hair	Life force, inspiration, connection of cosmos and soul
Gold and silver chalice	Sun (mind) and Moon (soul) as sources of heavenly water
Flowing water	Cleansing, fertility, life energy
Heavenly globe with seven-pointed star	Venus, symbol of the power of love
Light violet color	Cosmic intelligence
Large star with spiral haze	Star of Babylon, source of spiritual light, divine love
Smaller blue star	Earthly love
Crystals	Protection, healing power, crystalline clarity
Roses	Love, fertility
Butterflies	Renewal, lightness
Kabbalah: He ה	Window
Astrology: Aquarius ≈	Farsightedness, vision, higher viewpoint

GENERAL: Good prospects, hope, trust in the future, harmony, higher guidance

PROFESSION: Promising projects, setting the course for one's profession, following one's calling, beginning a propitious career

CONSCIOUSNESS: Deep insight and trust in cosmic laws

PARTNERSHIP: Promising relationship, mutual plans for the future, hopeful encounter, inspiring love

ENCOURAGES: Trusting in the good graces of the hour and approaching the future with hope

WARNS AGAINST: Getting too involved in the future and missing out on the present as a result

XVII

AS CARD FOR THE DAY: Welcome this day—the stars are favorable for you. Let yourself be inspired by a dream of the future. Whatever you begin promises to take a pleasant course, even in the long run, because today you have the necessary instinct for coming developments. In case you don't have any new plans, it would also be worthwhile cleaning up any old ones. You will be amazed at what comes to light as a result. This may also indicate memories that lead you to new visions.

AS CARD FOR THE YEAR: This year stands under a good star in the truest sense of the word. Make your plans for the future and risk a new beginning in which you set long-term goals. Above all, if you have a crisis or difficult phase behind you, the time has now come for new hope and trend-setting vision. This applies particularly, but not exclusively, to the area of love and partnership. Clear away the old rubble, wash your wounds in healing waters, and consider your situation from a higher perspective. You could even consider this to be a bird's-eye view. You will see joyful prospects that open up for you. Notice how promising your possibilities are. You can also use this year for inner cleansing and spiritual growth. Bring your life into harmony with cosmic order.

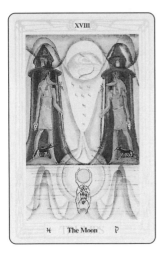

XVIII THE MOON

Symbolism	Meaning
Two black watchtowers	Gateway of fear, constriction, gateway to rebirth
Path between the towers	Path to wholeness
Two jackal-headed figures with black dogs	Guardians of the threshold, incorruptible guards who only let those without blame pass through
Scarabus with Sun	Resurrection, awaking consciousness, sunrise
Sky-blue mountains	Nut's thigh (she is goddess of the heavens and gives birth to the Sun from her vagina every morning)
Moon crescent facing downward	Sinister forces of the Moon, such as mental derangement, possession, obsession, madness
Nine drops of blood in the form of the Hebrew letter ' Yod	Ambivalent forces that emanate from the waning Moon
Oscillation curves in area of unconscious mind	Dreams as creative potential
Kabbalah: Koph ק	Back of the head
Astrology: Pisces ♓	Last sign of the zodiac, which leads to the new birth of the year

GENERAL: Fear of the threshold before an important step, feelings of insecurity, nightmares, stage fright, threatening memories, dark premonitions

PROFESSION: Critical phases, insecure job, fear of failure, intrigues, fraud, fear of examinations

CONSCIOUSNESS: Understanding the meaning of fear in showing the way

PARTNERSHIP: Unclear circumstances, unreliable or uncanny relationship, gnawing jealousy, becoming insecure, fear of an important step

ENCOURAGES: Overcoming the threshold of fear to reach the new land behind it

WARNS AGAINST: Getting lost in the dark, fleeing into illusion and states of intoxication, failing at the threshold

XVIII

AS CARD FOR THE DAY: Perhaps you already woke up from a nightmare this morning or have had a strange feeling about today for some other reason. Don't let yourself be irritated by any dreadful spectres. Even if you feel oppressed in the face of the demands on you today, or if your environment makes you feel insecure, don't avoid them. Be aware that there is an important and enriching experience waiting for you behind every threshold of fear. You can only have this experience when you overcome the obstacle. So encounter this day as alertly as possible and, despite any fears, cautiously and prudently go your way. You will be astonished at how much you can achieve as a result.

AS CARD FOR THE YEAR: There is a bottleneck you must get through this year. Or, despite all the adversities, there may be an important development whose birth you should assist. If this enterprise succeeds, the result will be delightful. However, the path that leads to this result is not simple, and is usually filled with fear. Don't let yourself be irritated by these fears. Even if ghosts sneak in during the night to plague you with nightmares, don't let yourself be intimidated. However, it wouldn't be smart to play things down or flatter yourself about the difficulties connected with your plans. Take the risks seriously, without letting yourself become discouraged. Consider precisely what you want to do and take one step after the other in a decisive and well-considered way, without letting this turn into a forced march. Don't feel obligated to play the hero.

XIX THE SUN

SYMBOLISM	MEANING
Radiant Sun	Joy of life, overcoming fears and worries, clarity
Sun-rose blossoming in the center	Union of masculine principle (Sun) with feminine principle (rose)
Dancing twin children with butterfly wings	Lightness, spontaneous joy, overcoming differences, inner fellowship
Rose-cross at the children's feet	Harmony between divine consciousness and earthly existence
Rainbow-colored ellipse with zodiac	Perfection, the great whole, harmony between conscious and unconscious mind
Green mountain	Mountain of paradise, fertile soil
Red wall	The peak of unity is near but not yet achieved
Kabbalah: Resh ר	Head
Astrology: Sun ☉	Courage in life, confidence

GENERAL: Happiness, enjoying the sunny side of life, new birth, high spirits, success, self-development, steering toward a culminating point

PROFESSION: Success, overcoming difficulties, power of conviction, creativity, enjoyment of work, promising plans for the future, good teamwork, self-realization

CONSCIOUSNESS: Finding life's joys in the original carefree state

PARTNERSHIP: Enjoying love, reconciliation, new beginning, happy times, deep trust, generously pampering each other

ENCOURAGES: Striving for a culmination, a peak, a high goal, in a self-confident and optimistic way

XIX

WARNS AGAINST: Naive overestimation of one's capabilities, recklessness, or wearing down one's powers

AS CARD FOR THE DAY: Today is a sunny day that you can enjoy to the fullest. You may experience it with a light heart or even celebrate a personal triumph. As self-confident and strong as you feel today, you can naturally also risk doing something new. With your positive charisma and self-assured manner, you can motivate other people and win them for yourself. Bask in your success and allow yourself and others to enjoy the good in life.

AS CARD FOR THE YEAR: In this year, you will probably walk on the sunny side of life. Whatever self-doubts and fears may have plagued you, these are now part of the past. Instead, you develop self-confidence, high spirits, and optimism. Time and time again, you will enjoy being at the focus of things. While life blesses you with riches, you will also encounter others who are generous and warm. Your openness brings appreciation from others and helps you achieve success and fulfillment in work and personal life. If you are grateful and happy about this, without becoming conceited as a result, then you will avoid being overbearing or arrogant.

The Aeon

XX THE AEON

SYMBOLISM	MEANING
Blue female body arched in the form of a uterus	Nut, Egyptian goddess of the heavens, who swallows the Sun in the evening and gives birth to it anew in the morning
Red, winged fireball	Hadit, the Goddess of Heaven's mate
Union of Nut and Hadit	The new age, whose representative is seen in Horus as the double deity, is born
Horus, the Sun god, as a double figure	Extroverted and introverted aspect of the Sun force
Horus, the elder, in the background as a crowned falcon god on the pharaoh's throne	Solidified power, external splendor, grandeur
Horus, the child (Harpokrates), in the foreground with a side curl and Uraeus snakes	The young, still tender and unspent force, overcoming old structures
Index finger on the mouth	Initiation through silence
Three-pronged Hebrew letter Shin ש with human figures	Child, adult, and old man, meaning that all periods of life participate in the new age
Kabbalah: Shin ש	Tooth
Astrology: Element of fire △	Purifying, confident force

GENERAL: Transformation, new beginning, hope, self-discovery, spiritual development

PROFESSION: Steps showing the right direction, reorganization, being open to new methods of work, advanced education, bringing a new spirit to one's working life

CONSCIOUSNESS: Being captured by the spirit of the new age

PARTNERSHIP: Trying out something new, stimulating impulses, renewal of existing relationships, new love, addition to the family

ENCOURAGES: Opening up to a new development and carefully advancing it

XX

WARNS AGAINST: Underestimating initial difficulties

AS CARD FOR THE DAY: You should emphasize new aspects today. This may relate to your outer appearance, or to fundamental things in your everyday life or environment. Get rid of what is outdated and let a fresh wind blow through the dusty realms. Don't cling to outmoded traditions. Stop staking your hopes on something that only appears to be time-tested. Instead, open up to new developments and trends that will prevail in the future.

AS CARD FOR THE YEAR: A completely new era of your life will begin this year. This may be the discovery or development of interests and abilities that have been concealed up to now. Or it may be a decisive and expansive step of consciousness; or a major change in your personal environment. You may move to another city (or even another country), or take on new assignments in terms of your profession. Or you may connect with interesting, open-minded people who now enter your life. Be receptive to this trendsetting chapter of your story, for it leads to a new future. In the initial stage of transition, leave the old structures behind and don't strain yourself with expectations that are too high. Carefully cultivate the seedlings of the new by leaving enough time and space for them to grow in a healthy manner.

The Universe

XXI THE UNIVERSE

SYMBOLISM	MEANING
Virginal, dancing goddess	Joy of life, force that produces life
Snake	Life (Aesculap staff), death (snake of paradise), and regeneration
Dance	Overcoming enmity between the snake and the woman, provoked by the "Fall of Man" and God's curse
Shining eye	Cosmic law, perception
Opened cosmic vulva	Origin of all Creation
Green source	Fertility, hope
Ring of stars consisting of 72 circles	The totality of Creation, stars = universe, 72 is the symbolic number for "all peoples"
Temple sketch (in lower portion)	Blueprint of Creation
Four water-spitting cherubim	The liveliness of Creation
Wheel implied at center	Beginning of the (Kabbalistic) Tree of Life
Kabbalah: Tau ת	Sign of the Cross
Astrology: Saturn ♄	The structure of reality

GENERAL: Completion, joy of living, being at the right place at the right time, resting in one's center, fulfillment, return home, reconciliation

PROFESSION: Enjoyment of work, finding one's calling, reaching the goal, being lively and creative

CONSCIOUSNESS: Looking at the whole, being one in the beginning and the end

PARTNERSHIP: Unconditional, living love, reconciling, sexual union and fulfillment, finding the right partner

ENCOURAGES: Taking one's place and enjoying life

WARNS AGAINST: Believing one has reached the goal

XXI

AS CARD FOR THE DAY: You feel especially lively today and are at peace with yourself and the world. Either things work out well on their own or you are not disturbed by possible disruptive factors. Enjoy the day by letting your soul relax and totally enjoy the paradisiac feeling. You could also use the opportunity to reduce any hostilities. Show yourself to be reconciliatory and create peace. This will fill you with great joy.

AS CARD FOR THE YEAR: During this year, you will have the opportunity to find your place in the world—a place full of happiness and joy. This may turn out to be your true home or, in the figurative sense, a friendship or love relationship where you feel safe and secure in the emotional sense. You will completely and totally enjoy this homecoming. This may also be a step that develops more consciousness, which brings you to your spiritual home, to your emotional center. Like a puzzle, the individual pieces of your life will connect harmoniously, gradually letting you see the meaningful whole. This order will also be translated into your everyday life as a feeling of harmony with yourself and the world.

ACE OF WANDS

Symbolism	Meaning
Torch	Creative force, sexual potency, illuminating power
10 flames	Potential of all 10 cards in the Wand series is found in the Ace
Green lightning bolts	Energy discharge, high tension, surprise, hope
Red background	Temperament, momentum in life
Number and Element	Opportunity (Ace = 1) for self-fulfillment (fire)
Astrology: The fire signs: Aries (♈), Leo (♌), Sagittarius (♐)	Initiative (♈), joy of life (♌), growth (♐)

GENERAL: Hopeful new beginning, initiative, willpower, decisiveness, electrifying idea, surge of creativity, opportunity for self-development, becoming inflamed about something

PROFESSION: Desire to do new projects, becoming self-employed, enjoyment of risks, growing through a challenge

CONSCIOUSNESS: Recognizing that self-fulfillment requires a willingness to take risks

PARTNERSHIP: New beginning, revival, the fire of love, turbulent encounter, passionate sexuality

ENCOURAGES: Initiative and decisive progress

WARNS AGAINST: Hot-headedness, impatience, and arrogance

AS CARD FOR THE DAY: Today you have the necessary energy to start something new, or you can put momentum back into something that has been bogged down. You encounter the challenges of the day with confidence and élan. Your high-spirited charisma has an effect on your surroundings and can also provide exciting moments in the interpersonal realm. Be ready for surprises, open yourself to impulses, and use opportunities that offer themselves to you.

TWO OF WANDS
DOMINION

Symbolism	Meaning
Two crossed Tibetan thunderbolts	Divine power that destroys and creates
Thunderbolt as phallus symbol	Procreative and aggressive sexual power
Demonic masks	Overcoming fear
Pair of snakes	Destruction and renewal
Six flames	Willpower that inflames through friction
Number and Element	Friction of (2) polar forces (fire)
Astrology: Mars (♂) in Aries (♈)	Forces of the ego, energy (♂) spirit of departure (♈)

GENERAL: Eagerness to fight, courage, willingness to take risks, willpower, becoming inflamed about something, spontaneous assertion, violent forging ahead, inconsideration

PROFESSION: Rivaling with the competition, professional challenge, increased willingness to take risks, committed actions

CONSCIOUSNESS: Recognizing destructive processes as a precondition for creative phases

PARTNERSHIP: Desire to make conquests, charged atmosphere, suspenseful game between dominant and devout forces, macho behavior

ENCOURAGES: Risking something, asserting something, conquering something

WARNS AGAINST: Inconsiderate aggressiveness, destructive actions, and hollow demonstrations of power

AS CARD FOR THE DAY: You can hardly be slowed down in your drive to move forward today. You are even willing to rigorously clear possible obstacles out of the way. But if you are too intent upon getting everything, it may be that you will ultimately burn out and be left standing with empty hands. So don't try to assert yourself at all costs. Instead, direct your fiery energy toward a worthwhile goal, or attempt to find a suitable outlet for your excessive power. For example, you could let off steam in sweat-producing sports or in playful competition with others.

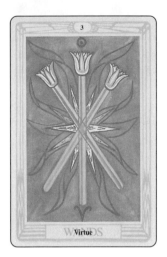

THREE OF WANDS
VIRTUE

SYMBOLISM	MEANING
Three blossoming yellow lotus wands	Blossoming vitality, sunlight
Ten-rayed white fire star at the center	The great creative force that supports growth, purity
Yellow-orange background	Morning light, sunrise, glory
Number and Element	Living (3) development (fire)
Astrology: Sun (☉) in Aries (♈)	Self-confidence, being centered, vitality (☉) in connection with a pioneering spirit and an urge to move forward (♈)

GENERAL: Healthy basis, confidence, success, initiative, vitality

PROFESSION: Helpful contacts, promising business connections, advantageous perspectives, good progress, support

CONSCIOUSNESS: Becoming aware of one's possibilities and developing confidence

PARTNERSHIP: Springtime feelings, forming delicate bonds, promising relationship, being together in a vital way, harmony

ENCOURAGES: Confidently looking into the future and tackling new goals

WARNS AGAINST: Impetuously overshooting the goal

AS CARD FOR THE DAY: Enjoy the springtime atmosphere of this day, no matter what the season may be. Shake off any gloomy thoughts and give yourself a bouquet. If you don't already have a steady relationship, you now feel with special intensity how ready you are for a new love. Perhaps there will actually be an opportunity to flirt today. But even if you are alone, you will still experience this day as extremely pleasant.

FOUR OF WANDS
COMPLETION

SYMBOLISM	MEANING
Yellow circle with four crossed wands over an eight-armed flaming Sun	Striving (8) from the earthly (4 and cross) to the divine (circle), completion (circle), and, at the same time, limitation (cross) of the creative force (Sun)
Ram's head (battle) and dove (peace) on the tips of the wands	Balance of opposites, harmonious togetherness
Deep-green background	Thriving, naturalness, joy of life
Number and Element	Solidified (4) will (fire)
Astrology: Venus (♀) in Aries (♈)	Charm and accommodation (♀) in balanced combination with a fighting spirit and desire to conquer (♈)

GENERAL: Order and harmony, balanced dynamics, self-assurance, equilibrium

PROFESSION: Distribution of profits, payment for work done, visible results, dynamic team spirit, efficiency

CONSCIOUSNESS: Insight into totality, which includes opposites

PARTNERSHIP: Being complemented by one's partner, harmonious togetherness, resolving conflicts, enriching encounters, sexual fulfillment, healthy dynamics in relationship

ENCOURAGES: The right mixture of accommodation and an uncompromising attitude

WARNS AGAINST: Burying even healthy tensions beneath compromises

AS CARD FOR THE DAY: Whatever you tackle today has a good chance of reaching a happy conclusion. You may even succeed at bringing together differences that previously appeared to be insurmountable. This will fill you with deep satisfaction. Despite all this, you still show yourself willing to make compromises, without losing sight of your own interests. If you have been postponing something unpleasant, such as a difficult phone conversation, today is the day to successfully take care of it.

FIVE OF WANDS
STRIFE

Symbolism	Meaning
Upright standing wand with ancient Egyptian royal symbol	Highest power
Violet blossoms and wings	Spiritual force
Two crossed wands with Phoenix heads	Creative, purifying energy
Two crossed wands with lotus blossoms	Receptive force, fertility
Ten-rayed star of flames	Heat that feeds itself from the friction of opposing energies
Sun-yellow background	Striving for light
Number and Element	Challenge (5) to competition (fire)
Astrology: Saturn (♄) in Leo (♌)	Courage (♌) to be responsible (♄) and persistent (♄) self-development (♌)

GENERAL: Comparison of strength, ambition, aggressiveness, challenge, over-stepping bounds

PROFESSION: Competition, differing business interests, persistently fighting out positions, ambitious commitment, struggling to win new territory

CONSCIOUSNESS: Thoroughly discussing controversial standpoints in order to find the best solution

PARTNERSHIP: Making one's peace, clashing with each other, bringing together differences

ENCOURAGES: Risking something new and facing the competition

WARNS AGAINST: Inconsiderate ambition and making a cocky display of oneself

AS CARD FOR THE DAY: This day promises to bring some excitement with it. Someone could get in your way, whereby differing interests will clash with each other. Don't avoid the conflict, but grab the bull by the horns and clearly show that you are someone to be reckoned with. If you remain fair and give it all you've got, you have a good chance of achieving a convincing solution. Even if you have to battle with bureaucrats today, you shouldn't hesitate to show your combative side.

SIX OF WANDS
VICTORY

Symbolism	Meaning
Phoenix heads	Creative power
Lotus blossoms	Receptive force
Winged Sun disks with snakes	Symbol of balanced rulership
Harmoniously crossed pairs of wands, at the intersection of which nine flames burn	Stabilized energy, crowning culmination
Violet background	Truth, noble-mindedness
Number and Element	Successful (6) battle (fire)
Astrology: Jupiter (♃) in Leo (♌)	Abundance, wealth, success (♃) in connection with self-assurance, self-fulfillment, strength, triumph (♌)

GENERAL: Reward for accomplished effort, good news, optimism, victory

PROFESSION: Recognition, encouraging success, successful conclusion, good business dealings, career leap, raise in pay, distinction

CONSCIOUSNESS: Developing optimism in life

PARTNERSHIP: Overcoming difficulties, warm and blossoming relationship, pleasant prospects

ENCOURAGES: Trusting that everything will go well

WARNS AGAINST: Condescendingly flaunting one's success

AS CARD FOR THE DAY: You have every reason to be joyful because today is your lucky day! There is good news in the air. Especially if you have a strenuous phase behind you, you will now notice how quickly things progress and that you have moved to the fast lane. Wherever you have made good effort, recognition and reward will be waiting for you. Enjoy this triumph, show your joy, and celebrate appropriately with friends.

SEVEN OF WANDS
VALOUR

SYMBOLISM	MEANING
Vertical club in the foreground	Wild elemental force, hero's weapon
Three harmoniously crossed pairs of wands with Phoenix heads, lotus blossoms, and winged Sun disks in the background	Orderly forces whose effect is gradually fading
Flame without direction	Wasted, aimless energy
Dark violet background	Threat
Number and Element	Risky (7) self-assertion (fire)
Astrology: Mars ($\male$) in Leo ($\leo$)	Courage, decisiveness, and willingness to engage in conflict ($\male$) in connection with self-confidence certain of success ($\leo$)

GENERAL: Risking a single-handed effort, growing beyond one's own limitations, struggling with difficulties, taking a risk

PROFESSION: Endangered position, hard assignment, decisively standing up for a plan—alone, if necessary

CONSCIOUSNESS: Courageously exerting oneself for a good but waning (or unpopular) cause

PARTNERSHIP: Saving the relationship from failing or turning away a threat to it through a daring step, having the commitment to bring new momentum into a tired relationship

ENCOURAGES: Bravely rescuing an apparently lost cause

WARNS AGAINST: Overestimation of one's abilities and meaningless waste of energy

AS CARD FOR THE DAY: A victory that you had already counted as yours could be endangered today, or an important matter that may suddenly lose its significance. Check out the other people getting involved in your affairs in order to compete with you for your position. Don't just watch without taking action when all your hopes threaten to be dashed, but fight resolutely for your concerns. If necessary, risk taking action on your own.

EIGHT OF WANDS
SWIFTNESS

SYMBOLISM	MEANING
Eight red wand bolts in front of a three-dimensional octahedron	Eight, the mediator number, lets the flashes of inspiration from higher worlds penetrate into our (three-dimensional) reality, sudden perception, breakthrough to freedom, tension turns into light
Rainbow	Bridge from spiritual to earthly world
Light-blue background	Spiritual revelation, intelligence
Number and Element	Courage (fire) to make changes (8)
Astrology: Mercury (☿) in Sagittarius (♐)	Confident, farsighted, hopeful (♐) thinking and perceiving (☿)

GENERAL: "Aha" experience, sudden solution to problems, flashes of inspiration, being a "live wire"

PROFESSION: Innovation, electrifying ideas, favorable developments, new business contacts, foreign business deals, advanced education, taking quick action

CONSCIOUSNESS: Setting off for new inner horizons by overcoming old thought patterns

PARTNERSHIP: Love at first sight, sudden resolution of conflicts, animating impulses, highly charged eroticism

ENCOURAGES: Opening oneself for new perceptions and taking immediate action

WARNS AGAINST: Drawing premature conclusions, an excessively rational approach, intellectual exaltation of the mind

AS CARD FOR THE DAY: Some good news or an unexpected phone call could electrify you today and give the day a surprising turn of events. Your mind is "charged," and one of the many ideas chasing through your brain holds the solution for an old problem. Or perhaps a spark will kindle the fires of love? That would certainly be the most wonderful reason for the coming night to turn to day for you.

NINE OF WANDS
STRENGTH

SYMBOLISM	MEANING
Eight crossed arrows with tips pointing downward	Forces that activate the unconscious energies
Perpendicular center wand, connecting the Sun (☉) and the Moon (☽)	Harmony between conscious mind (☉) and unconscious mind (☽), harmonious interplay of mind (☉) and soul (☽)
Ten-rayed star in background	Illuminating power produced by the harmonious connection
Background getting lighter toward the top	Strength rising from the unconscious mind
Number and Element	Concentrated (9) courage (fire)
Astrology: Moon (☽) in Sagittarius (♐)	Confidence and urge to develop (♐) rising from the unconscious (☽)

GENERAL: Drawing on abundant resources, experiencing a flow of energy, anticipation, inspiration

PROFESSION: Reaching a new and promising level, trust in one's own abilities, beginning a plan with courage and commitment

CONSCIOUSNESS: Being inspired by the unconscious

PARTNERSHIP: Stability and harmony, animating emotional impulses, new powerful relationship, intensive exchange, enthusiasm

ENCOURAGES: Brave actions in trust of one's own intuition

WARNS AGAINST: Letting oneself be flooded by delusions of grandeur

AS CARD FOR THE DAY: Today you should trust yourself! Go against your grain and risk something that you haven't had the courage to do up until now. In doing so, you can put complete trust in your intuition and it will instinctively let you do the right thing. But you can also use the inspiring energy of this day to develop joyful visions for the future by planning something like your next vacation.

TEN OF WANDS
OPPRESSION

SYMBOLISM	MEANING
Eight flaming wands	Blazing impulses
Wild flames in the background	Uncontrolled energies
Orange-colored background	Fiery energies
Two powerful Tibetan ritual wands in foreground	Control and suppression of fiery energies
Number and Element	Sum (10) of aggressive forces (fire)
Astrology: Saturn (♄) in Sagittarius (♐)	Blockage, inhibition, suppression (♄) of enthusiasm, power of conviction, life philosophy, expansion (♐)

GENERAL: Blocked development, problems with authority, frustration, fear of life, "straitjacket"

PROFESSION: Intensive pressure because of overwork, stress, or badgering; failed struggle for recognition, fear of professional future, leadership problems

CONSCIOUSNESS: Mastering inner tensions through external efforts alone

PARTNERSHIP: Callousness, power struggles, fighting against taboos and prohibitions, blocked feelings, hopelessness

ENCOURAGES: Recognizing one's own limitations and acting responsibly

WARNS AGAINST: Demonstrations of power, intolerance, and suppressed aggressions

AS CARD FOR THE DAY: Arm yourself with a good portion of discipline and stamina today. You may very well need it. Perhaps you will be attacked because of your opinions, or someone will try to keep you in check. However, it may also be that you wind up in conflict with an authority, such as the boss or the traffic police. In no case should you let yourself be provoked. Instead, remain calm and composed, even if this is difficult for you to do. Afterward, you will recognize why this was a smart move.

Princess of Wands

PRINCESS OF WANDS

Symbolism	Meaning
Dynamically moving, yellow-green flames on a red background	Effervescent vital energy, powerful confidence, wild energies
Naked, feminine figure	Tempting purity
Ostrich plumes as headdress	Justice
Sun wand	Illuminating power
Tiger facing downward	Instincts splitting off
Golden altar with rams' heads	Fiery vital energy, force of springtime
Burning rose blossoms	Sacrifice to the goddess of love

GENERAL: Young, dynamic, impulsive, zestful woman; amazon, primer, impetuous new beginning, enthusiasm, desire for adventure, impatience

PROFESSION: Innovative ideas that urge their expression, beginning of professional career

CONSCIOUSNESS: Experiencing euphoria through bubbling high spirits

PARTNERSHIP: Feelings of springtime, stormy infatuation, sexual desire, exciting flirtation, flash in the pan, infidelity

ENCOURAGES: Living in a spontaneous and stimulating way

WARNS AGAINST: Theatrical behavior and moody impulsiveness

AS CARD FOR THE DAY: Today you want either all or nothing. You will not be satisfied with anything done in halves. In terms of your energy, you are in such suspense that you can hardly wait for the spark to catch fire. This could lead to a passionate love encounter. You are also ready to get involved in some kind of adventure, without thinking about the consequences. Today there is actually no reason for you not to completely let go of reason and act in keeping with the pleasure principle for once.

Prince of Wands

PRINCE OF WANDS

Symbolism	Meaning
Naked warrior on chariot	Strong instincts, power of assertion, youthfulness
Crown of rays	Radiance, creative force
Magical seal on his chest	Power and strength of influence
Fiery lion as draft animal	Impulse, forward-urging animalistic energy
Bridled lion	Mastering the instincts
Pointed flames	Creative, purposeful energy
Spear with Phoenix head	Egyptian symbol of rulership, purifying power

GENERAL: Daredevil, conqueror, hero, sprinter, hothead, new momentum, initiative, enthusiasm

PROFESSION: Readiness for action, enjoy taking risks, courage to be independent, pioneer spirit, starting something with much élan

CONSCIOUSNESS: Optimistic approach to life with increased self-assurance

PARTNERSHIP: Wild passion, demanding eroticism, dangerous adventure, spontaneous but childlike satisfaction of desire, unpredictable moods

ENCOURAGES: Encountering life in an open and totally self-confident manner.

WARNS AGAINST: Spontaneous satisfaction of desires at expense of long-term goals

AS CARD FOR THE DAY: For a truly intensive experience, you will also put up with risks today. It would best suit you to prove on all levels what kind of "character" you really are. But when you let go of the reins in the wrong place, you could easily run over someone with your brash approach. This could even cause problems with neighbors or colleagues. Seek the right stage for your performance. Set a new record for yourself, or go out and have fun.

QUEEN OF WANDS

SYMBOLISM	MEANING
Queen sitting on throne of flames with closed eyes	Inner fire, Kundalini energy, spirituality
Long hair	Vital force
Twelve-rayed crown with winged Sun	Fully developed creative power, enlightenment
Spear with pine cone (Thyros staff in cult of Dionysius)	Passion, ecstasy
Leopard	Animalistic forces, instinctual nature
Hand on head of the leopard	Careful taming and integration of animalistic forces

GENERAL: Healthy sense of self-assurance, initiative, openness, impulsiveness, independence, self-fulfillment; high-spirited, charismatic, generous woman who is mature in terms of human experience

PROFESSION: Confidently finding self-fulfillment in a profession, being a match for big assignments, becoming self-employed, assuming leadership responsibilities

CONSCIOUSNESS: Turning burning passion into spiritual striving

PARTNERSHIP: Equality, mature relationship, gentle submission, the Tantra of love, heartfelt warmth

ENCOURAGES: Expressing personal needs and standing up for oneself

WARNS AGAINST: Egocentrism and self-assertion at any cost

AS CARD FOR THE DAY: Today you call the tune! You feel strong, know exactly what you want, and are willing to even tackle difficult tasks on your own. Thanks to this decisiveness, you can now succeed in taking definitive steps. With your supremely independent conduct, you have a convincing effect on other people, who like to let you encourage, motivate, and guide them. However, it is also possible that a high-spirited, strong-willed woman will play an important role for you today.

KNIGHT OF WANDS

Knight of Wands

SYMBOLISM	MEANING
Knight with armor and mantle of flames on rearing horse	Creative, upward-shooting but controlled power
Black horse with one horn	Instinctual force, decisiveness, and focused energy that is directed at a goal
Burning torch	Bringing light and new vision into the world; strength, kindling a fire even in others
Blazing flame	Energy, passion
Yellow background with rays	Enlightenment, perception

GENERAL: Self-confidence, courage, striving for ideals, strong enterprising spirit; strong-willed, dynamic mature man; exemplary personality, leader nature

PROFESSION: Leadership qualities, motivation for new projects, pioneer work, supreme independence, working in a confident and self-reliant manner

CONSCIOUSNESS: Focusing one's willpower on high goals

PARTNERSHIP: Two equal partners being together in a high-spirited way, generosity, the will to have constructive conflicts, a dynamic relationship

ENCOURAGES: Decisive, goal-oriented, and courageous actions

WARNS AGAINST: Conceit, intolerance, and egoism

AS CARD FOR THE DAY: Today is the day to be ready for anything! You sparkle with energy and can hardly wait to infect others with your enthusiasm. You know exactly what you want, set your sights on high goals, and have a good chance of achieving these. Things that are a great effort for others you take can care of with your little finger. But despite all this enthusiasm and confidence, you should be careful not to inconsiderately walk all over others. You may also encounter an interesting, high-spirited man today.

Ace of Cups

ACE OF CUPS

SYMBOLISM	MEANING
Grail chalice	Love, openness, devotion, search for fulfillment, healing
Chalice in blue colors of the Virgin Mary	Mercy, grace, empathy
White lotus that bears the chalice	The forces that nourish the chalice and fill it with the water of life
Two lotus blossoms within each other that only bloom in the next card (2 of Cups)	Beauty, happiness, and joy as the potential that will develop
Ray of light falling from above	Inspiring creative spirit
Number and Element	Opportunity (Ace = 1) for finding fulfillment (water)
Astrology: The water signs: Cancer (♋), Scorpio (♏), Pisces (♓)	Emotional depth (♋), emotional strength (♏), devotion and empathy (♓)

GENERAL: Bliss, inner wealth, openness, harmony, opportunity to find fulfillment

PROFESSION: Opportunity for finding the true calling, meaningful activity, professional fulfillment, peace and contentment at place of work

CONSCIOUSNESS: Opening up to the mystery of all-encompassing love

PARTNERSHIP: Experiencing deep love, finding great fulfillment, romantic moods, devotion

ENCOURAGES: Using an opportunity for finding great happiness

WARNS AGAINST: Starry-eyed daydreaming

AS CARD FOR THE DAY: You will receive grist for your mill today. Take time by the hands so you can risk something you think promises fulfillment. Good opportunities offer themselves, especially in matters of the heart. If you openly approach other people and let yourself be guided by your inner voice, you may actually walk directly into the arms of great happiness. Perhaps you may find peace of mind by overcoming an old problem or finally burying a hatchet.

TWO OF CUPS
LOVE

SYMBOLISM	MEANING
Overflowing chalices	Exuberant love
Intertwined, water-sprouting fish	Loving union, emotional and physical connection, power of attraction, emotional exchange
Two blossomed lotus flowers connected with each other	Harmonious development, happy connection of two poles, love
Calm water, blue sky	Peace and harmony
Number and Element	Merging (water) of opposites (2)
Astrology: Venus (♀) in Cancer (♋)	Loving, delightful (♀) devotion and feelings (♋) of emotional (♋) connection (♀)

GENERAL: Happy relationship, cooperation, reconciliation, joyful encounter

PROFESSION: Good working climate, trusting teamwork, pleasant contact with clients/customers, entering into a business partnership

CONSCIOUSNESS: Uniting the two souls within oneself

PARTNERSHIP: Loving encounter, partnership of souls, reconciliation, experiencing the love of one's life

ENCOURAGES: Connecting lovingly with others

WARNS AGAINST: Betraying one's principles because of a craving for harmony

AS CARD FOR THE DAY: Today the heart is trump! The day stands completely under the star of deep sympathy, deep love, or a reconciliation. Set your emotional antenna on reception. Perhaps you will fall in love anew. If you already are in a stable relationship, then you may experience a second springtime in it. But don't wait until someone delivers great happiness to your doorstep for you. Instead, you can make your contribution so that Fortuna can give you her gifts and Cupid's arrows don't miss the mark.

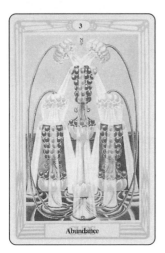

THREE OF CUPS
ABUNDANCE

SYMBOLISM	MEANING
Overflowing chalices	Love, joy, and abundance that let the heart overflow
Pomegranates that form the chalices	Fertility, deep dependence or attachment[4]
Golden lotus blossoms that fill the chalices	Spiritual love
Deep-blue water, from which the lotus stems grow	Original source of fertility
Number and Element	Living (3) feelings (water)
Astrology: Mercury (☿) in Cancer (♋)	Emotional (♋) exchange (☿), emotional (♋) intelligence (☿)

[4]Because she ate the seed of a pomegranate, Persephone had to remain in the underworld as Hades' spouse.

GENERAL: Fulfillment, joy, fertile exchange, gratitude, well-being, rich harvest

PROFESSION: Pleasant business dealings, good teamwork, joy in working, promising projects, contracts with good prospects

CONSCIOUSNESS: Being filled with deep gratitude

PARTNERSHIP: Happiness in love, harmonious togetherness, fruitful relationship, wedding

ENCOURAGES: Celebrating the occasions when they occur

WARNS AGAINST: Distributing the harvest before it is brought in

AS CARD FOR THE DAY: Welcome today since it will give you many gifts. Enjoy the lovely aspects of life, draw on all your resources, and show that you are thankful for the amenities that life is now giving you. It's best to share your joy with others. Invite good friends over, enjoy a pleasant time with your family, or pamper someone you love. After all, it isn't every day that you have so many reasons to celebrate.

FOUR OF CUPS
LUXURY

SYMBOLISM	MEANING
Filled chalices	Wealth of feelings, emotional satiation
Square pedestal	Stable basis
Strongly rooted, red lotus that pours itself over the chalices	Overflowing love, deep feelings, sense of emotional security
Black-gray sky, restless waters	Deep-lying, as yet unconscious restlessness
Number and Element	Emotional (water) satiety (4)
Astrology: Moon (☽) in Cancer (♋)	Caring, motherly, devoted (♋) feelings (☽)

GENERAL: Reveling, enjoying life, emotional security, sense of security

PROFESSION: Familiar work climate, having a good time, pleasant business dealings, well-established team

CONSCIOUSNESS: Recognizing the seed of decay that abundance bears within itself

PARTNERSHIP: Enjoying love to the full, pampering others and letting oneself be pampered, experiencing a sense of security within the family, being together in a caring way

ENCOURAGES: Drawing on all of one's resources and enjoying the moment

WARNS AGAINST: The naive belief that everything will stay this good

AS CARD FOR THE DAY: Take the time to really enjoy this day. You have achieved a temporary culmination and have every reason to take a well-deserved break. Totally enjoy yourself and don't struggle with problems that you can also solve tomorrow, if they haven't solved themselves on their own by then. Instead, be happy about the sympathy and attention that you are now experiencing. Since life has given you so many gifts, you can also show others your own generosity.

FIVE OF CUPS
DISAPPOINTMENT

Symbolism	Meaning
Empty chalices and dried-out lake	Withered feelings, disillusionment, infertility
Two wilted lotus blossoms	Faded love
Chalices arranged as reversed pentagram	Victory of matter over spirit
Lotus roots in form of butterfly	Power of transformation
Blue-red sky	Anger, danger
Number and Element	Emotional (water) crisis (5)
Astrology: Mars (♂) in Scorpio (♏)	Power (♂) growing from decay (♏)

GENERAL: Disappointed expectations, faded hope, melancholy, painful perceptions, transformational crisis

PROFESSION: Disappointed projects, business losses, sudden cancellation, failure

CONSCIOUSNESS: Recognizing the power of renewal that grows from decay

PARTNERSHIP: Dying feelings, getting "bogged down" in a relationship, the beginning of the end

ENCOURAGES: Showing one's worries and disappointment

WARNS AGAINST: Blind optimism and exaggerated expectations

AS CARD FOR THE DAY: You may deal with a rap on the knuckles today. Something that you were already looking forward to, or had hoped for in a very matter-of-course manner, will not fulfill your expectations. If it's just a quite minor detail, take it with humor. But if something truly valuable falls apart, then bear it with composure without concealing your disappointment. The more consciously and honestly you confront your failed hopes, the more likely you will be to feel the ground beneath your feet again.

SIX OF CUPS
PLEASURE

Symbolism	Meaning
Filled chalices	Fulfillment, contentment
"Dancing" orange-colored lotus blossoms	Joy of life, vitality, ease
Lotus stems in butterfly motion	New life awakens, liberated forces
Moving waters	Revived feelings
Light-blue sky	Peacefulness, contemplation
Number and Element	Emotional (water) relationship (6)
Astrology: Sun (☉) in Scorpio (♏)	Deep, self-renewing (♏) joy of life (☉)

GENERAL: Reawakening spirits, drawing from the depths, finding fulfillment, emotional recovery, well-being

PROFESSION: Great creative power, enjoyment of work, pleasant assignments

CONSCIOUSNESS: Finding one's center

PARTNERSHIP: Blossoming of feelings, deep happiness, sensual pleasure, sexual fulfillment

ENCOURAGES: Opening up to life and its joys from the bottom of one's heart

WARNS AGAINST: Gluttony and greed

AS CARD FOR THE DAY: Today you have every reason to do a dance of joy! No matter whether you do it in the actual sense or are just inwardly moved, don't hold back. Show that you feel well in every way. If you sense that you have been reborn after a difficult phase, you should once again completely enjoy the sweetness of life. Celebrate with others or just yourself. Fulfill a wish that you have long had.

SEVEN OF CUPS
DEBAUCH

Symbolism	Meaning
Seven chalices arranged in two descending triangles	Decay
Tiger lilies fill the chalices with poisonous nectar	Deceptive, sinister seduction
Muddy, poisoned lake	Danger of destruction
Gray-green sky	Poisoned atmosphere
Number and Element	Dangerous (7) deceptions (water)
Astrology: Venus (♀) in Scorpio (♏)	Depths (♏) of desire (♀), pleasure (♀) that leads to dependence (♏)

GENERAL: Disaster, dangerous temptation, addictions, deception, threatening calamity

PROFESSION: Intrigues, tainted business negotiations, failed ventures, fatal dependencies

CONSCIOUSNESS: Learning to differentiate between the quest and addiction

PARTNERSHIP: Poisoned atmosphere, bondage, being drawn into bad society or dirty business deals through the relationship

ENCOURAGES: Leaving something as it is

WARNS AGAINST: Flight from reality and tempting steps that lead to depravity

AS CARD FOR THE DAY: Don't let yourself be tempted by even the most enticing offer today. You could easily wind up in a swamp of deceptive hopes, from which it will be difficult to extract yourself. Avoid unclear situations and everything that is morbid or impenetrable. It's better to do without something that may be very appealing but only brings short-term advantages. Stay wide-awake, and be especially careful around alcohol and other drugs.

EIGHT OF CUPS
INDOLENCE

Symbolism	Meaning
Damaged chalices, of which only half are filled	Attrition, insufficient vitality
Moldy, dark sea	Melancholy, danger of going under
Wilted lotus blossoms	Lack of strength and energy
Darkened, clouded sky	Depression, threat, fear of future
Number and Element	Changing (8) moods (water)
Astrology: Saturn (♄) in Pisces (♓)	Hardened, dead (♄) feelings (♓)

GENERAL: Weakness, broken hopes, disheartenment, resignation, necessity of changing one's ways, stagnation, depression

PROFESSION: Poisoned work atmosphere, stagnant business dealings, lacking energy, disappointed expectations, endangered job, mismanagement

CONSCIOUSNESS: Recognizing one's own errors that have led to disappointment

PARTNERSHIP: Deadened feelings, trouble brewing, lack of commitment, hopeless relationship, resignation

ENCOURAGES: Leaving the disastrous morass

WARNS AGAINST: Clinging to what has decayed or starting something with no prospects of success

AS CARD FOR THE DAY: Things could get quite messy today. Even if this isn't solely your fault, you still have contributed toward it. Since the matter is quite muddled, you should attempt to free yourself from this morass as quickly as possible. However, it is important to find out what has led to this standstill. This is the only way you can avoid succumbing to this same mistake in the future.

NINE OF CUPS
HAPPINESS

Symbolism	Meaning
Lotus blossoms pour water into nine chalices	Overflowing joy
Arrangement in form of even rectangle	Stability
Blue sky	Confidence, peace
Calm sea	Stable feelings, balance
Number and Element	Collected (9) feelings (water)
Astrology: Jupiter (4) in Pisces ($\mathcal{H}$)	Happiness, growth, trust (4) in spirituality and all-encompassing love ($\mathcal{H}$)

GENERAL: Bliss, optimism, meaningful experience, charity, trust in God, quiet happiness

PROFESSION: Enjoyment of work, happy touch in business deals, team spirit, advantageous conclusion of contract

CONSCIOUSNESS: Joy that lets the heart overflow

PARTNERSHIP: Happiness in love, warmheartedness, deep affection, emotional and physical fulfillment

ENCOURAGES: Being happy about one's good luck and looking to the future in a spirit of trust

WARNS AGAINST: Sugary pompousness

AS CARD FOR THE DAY: It's all very well to laugh today because luck is on your side! Things have taken a very delightful course and develop completely to your advantage. Make something of it. You can even increase your joy by letting others participate in it. Go on a little outing with your family or invite friends over. You can naturally also use today's tailwind to easily take care of some things that you have long wanted to be done with.

TEN OF CUPS
SATIETY

SYMBOLISM	MEANING
Chalices arranged as Tree of Life[5]	Emotional harmony, deep fulfillment
Swaying chalices	Beginning change, instability
Large, red lotus	Giving, all-encompassing love
Red background and handle made of ram's horns	Mars quality, fiery energy, setting off anew
Number and Element	Abundance (10) of feelings (water)
Astrology: Mars (♂) in Pisces (♓)	Fulfillment (♓) and a new beginning (♂), emotional (♓) strength (♂)

[5]Kabbalistic symbol depicting the totality of Creation.

GENERAL: Fulfillment, culmination, completion, gratitude, sociableness

PROFESSION: Successful work, good business transaction, positive working climate, retirement

CONSCIOUSNESS: Knowing that culmination puts an end to the ascent

PARTNERSHIP: Happy, fulfilled times; reveling in feelings; pampering each other

ENCOURAGES: Enjoying one's happiness together with others but not clinging to it

WARNS AGAINST: The possible decline that can follow a culmination

AS CARD FOR THE DAY: Celebrate the occasions as they occur! Today you will have good reason to do so. This may mean that you successfully complete something, are joyful and thankful about a result, or just simply feel completely content with yourself and life in general. Let yourself have something good, meet with friends, and enjoy this carefree feeling as long as it lasts.

Princess of Cups

PRINCESS OF CUPS

SYMBOLISM	MEANING
Dancing woman in shell-shaped dress	Concealed fascination, spacious inner world, mediality
Crystals forming	Crystallization of inner values
Chalice with turtle	Inner world that opens to the outside
Swan as crown	Prophetic gifts
Dolphins leaping pleasurably	Joy of life, creative power
White lotus	Divine connectedness

GENERAL: Sensitive young woman, enchanting seductress, dreamer, muse, longing for union, romance, deep feelings, daydreaming, quiet joy

PROFESSION: Good intuition in decisions related to profession, instinctively doing the right thing, trusting one's feelings in everyday working life

CONSCIOUSNESS: Having a medial experience

PARTNERSHIP: Two people gently and cautiously approaching each other, tender feelings of love, longing

ENCOURAGES: Opening up emotionally and expressing concealed feelings and desires

WARNS AGAINST: Seductive coquettishness and naive self-deception

AS CARD FOR THE DAY: Don't wonder if you are gripped by deep desires or filled with tender feelings of love today. More than usual, you are open today for romantic encounters, but also susceptible to seductions of all kinds. Be open for it since there's a good chance you will have an enchanting experience, letting previously concealed aspects of your being resonate within you.

Prince of Cups

PRINCE OF CUPS

Symbolism	Meaning
Naked warrior with eagle helmet	Maturation process, refinement of instinctual nature
Shell-shaped chariot, drawn by an eagle	Inspiring mental vigor that illuminates the waters of the unconscious mind
Chalice with snake	Transformation and renewal
Large lotus blossom	Emotional strength

GENERAL: Tender, romantic man; seducer, charmer, warm personality, gushing enthusiasm

PROFESSION: Successful connection between intuition and knowledge, social commitment, artistic activity, inner work

CONSCIOUSNESS: Being inspired by one's own feelings

PARTNERSHIP: Romantic and imaginative exchange, loving approach, the magic of love, crush

ENCOURAGES: Expressing one's feelings, or letting oneself be carried away by a flight of fancy

WARNS AGAINST: Simulated emotional gushing

AS CARD FOR THE DAY: Today will give wings to your soul! Not only will the head and heart harmonize joyfully well, but you may also experience an emotional lift that lets you reach seventh heaven. Use the opportunity to put things in order, since it's necessary to use the rational mind in addition to imagination. Above all, if something has become bogged down in the interpersonal realm, you should free it from this state today.

QUEEN OF CUPS

Symbolism	Meaning
Veiled, female figure	Mysterious oracle fairy
Calm sea	Unconscious, innermost feeling
Reflection	Mirror of the soul, the collective unconscious, dreams
Crab (in chalice)	Instinctive, individualistic approach
White shell chalice	Motherhood, reincarnation, purity
Lotus blossom	Effusive love, purity, receptiveness
Heron	Watchfulness, prudence, sure instincts
Blue-white arc of light	Intuition

GENERAL: Sensitivity, devotion, inspiration, depth of feeling, receptivity, mercy; intuition, maturity, an artistic woman

PROFESSION: Spiritual tasks, artistic inspiration, creative pause, medial and therapeutic activities

CONSCIOUSNESS: Listening to the inner voice and trusting it

PARTNERSHIP: Soulful, wordless understanding; soul mates, loving affection, devotion, deep feelings, longing for union

ENCOURAGES: Being true to one's feelings

WARNS AGAINST: Uncritically giving in to one's moods or getting lost in pure wishful thinking

AS CARD FOR THE DAY: Your emotional openness makes you especially receptive to the needs of your surrounding world today. However, at the same time you are also correspondingly vulnerable to possible harshness. But you should still trustingly approach others since your good intuition will protect you from difficulties. Pay special attention to your dreams! It may also be possible that a sympathetic woman enters your life today and brings you closer to the mysterious or enigmatic aspects of life.

KNIGHT OF CUPS

Knight of Cups

Symbolism	Meaning
Upward riding, winged knight	Inspired cerebral principle that climbs into spiritual spheres
White horse	Purified instinctual nature, purity
Green armor	Naturalness, hope, fertility
Crab (in chalice)	Sure instincts, individual approach, aggressiveness
Peacock spreading its tail	Water element's scintillating blaze of colors and magic of the emotional world

GENERAL: Emotional depth, artistic talent, medial abilities, imagination, sensitivity; mature, helpful, sensitive man; intuitive advisor

PROFESSION: Bringing work and one's own needs into harmony, making use of emotional forces in profession; tasks that demand intuition, imagination, and deep understanding; artistic and social activities

CONSCIOUSNESS: Being inspired by a goal that is within reach

PARTNERSHIP: Emotional openness, considerate togetherness, deep understanding, wealth of feelings

ENCOURAGES: A great leap toward a high objective

WARNS AGAINST: Running after a mirage

AS CARD FOR THE DAY: Today you should apply all your strength to a goal that is close at hand. Once again, show complete commitment in order to achieve it. More than usual, you will notice how intensely your feelings support you in doing so and how your lively imagination inspires you. However, a sensitive and sympathetic man may also enter your life or play an important role for you today. You will experience his proximity as very enriching and agreeable.

ACE OF SWORDS

SYMBOLISM	MEANING
Crown with 22 rays	Shining wisdom of the 22 major arcana
Penetrating green sword	Mental power that penetrates and perceives everything
θελημα (Greek *Thelema* = "will") as inscription on the blade	The will to direct the power of perception at the highest goals
Hilt with snake and two Moon crescents	The intellect as the bridge to the unconscious mind
Sunlight with crystal structures illuminating the sky	Spiritual enlightenment, awakening consciousness, illuminating insights
Number and Element	Opportunity (Ace = 1) of perceiving something or making an intelligent decision (air)
Astrology: The air signs: Gemini (♊), Libra (♎), Aquarius (♒)	Curiosity (♊), sociability (♎), intellect (♒)

GENERAL: Intellectual interests, thirst for knowledge, the power of reason, good opportunity to clarify something, making sensible and clear decisions

PROFESSION: Good ideas, analytical approach, designing new projects, finding solutions for professional problems, making well-considered decisions, career-planning

CONSCIOUSNESS: Making a decisive step toward self-knowledge

PARTNERSHIP: Clarification of problems and misunderstandings, clear circumstances and unambiguous decisions, important perceptions

ENCOURAGES: Clarifying, understanding, deciding something

WARNS AGAINST: Hair-splitting, or an approach that is too calculating

AS CARD FOR THE DAY: Today an electrifying idea helps you solve an annoying problem or suddenly understand something that has long been a puzzle for you. Be wide-awake and set all your antennas on reception. This will give you a grasp of things, as well as the opportunity to make a good decision or clarify something that should have been cleared up long ago.

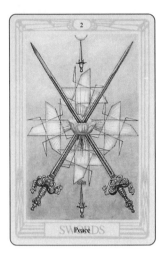

TWO OF SWORDS
PEACE

Symbolism	Meaning
Two crossed swords	Putting down the weapons
Blue, five-leafed rose blossom	Mercy, appeasement, peace
Even, white geometric pattern	Equilibrium, harmonious order, peace
Two small swords with crescent Moon and symbol for Libra	Balance, repose
Green-yellow background	Ambivalence
Number and Element	Reconciliatory (2) thoughts (air)
Astrology: Moon (☽) in Libra (♎)	Balanced, peaceful (♎) feelings (☽), need (☽) for harmony (♎)

GENERAL: State of balance, relaxation, serenity, thoughtfulness, fairness, compromise

PROFESSION: Clever business tactics, fair negotiations, balanced working day, resolving conflicts

CONSCIOUSNESS: Experiencing inner peace and harmony

PARTNERSHIP: Peaceful relationship, being together like partners, equal rights, harmony, reconciliation

ENCOURAGES: Fair, balanced solution for overcoming disputes

WARNS AGAINST: Implacability and sham peace

AS CARD FOR THE DAY: Today you should put your weapons down. A possible solution to a smoldering conflict will show up as a surprise. Don't hesitate to take the first step. Demonstrate that you are willing to negotiate and make a fair offer to the other party. But so that this doesn't turn into a sham peace, find a true compromise that puts no one at a disadvantage. If you smoke the peace pipe together afterward, you will feel more relaxed and content.

THREE OF SWORDS
SORROW

Symbolism	Meaning
Yellow rose with petals falling off	Loss of perfection
Mighty sword and two crooked swords	Powerful insight and added perceptions
Destruction of rose	Knowledge strikes the heart and destroys beauty and harmony
Dark, stormy background	Calamity brewing, fearful expectations, chaos
Number and Element	Secured (3) but unpleasant perceptions (air)
Astrology: Saturn (♄) in Libra (♎)	Blockage/end (♄) of peace and harmony (♎)

GENERAL: Bad news, disappointment, weakness, sorrow, helplessness, chaos, disillusionment, renunciation, loss

PROFESSION: Failure, threat of being fired, bankruptcy, miscalculation, not passing exam, ill tidings

CONSCIOUSNESS: Painful, sobering, but necessary insights

PARTNERSHIP: Pangs of love, fear of loss, injuries, end of relationship, failed hope

ENCOURAGES: Opening up to an unwelcome but totally necessary insight

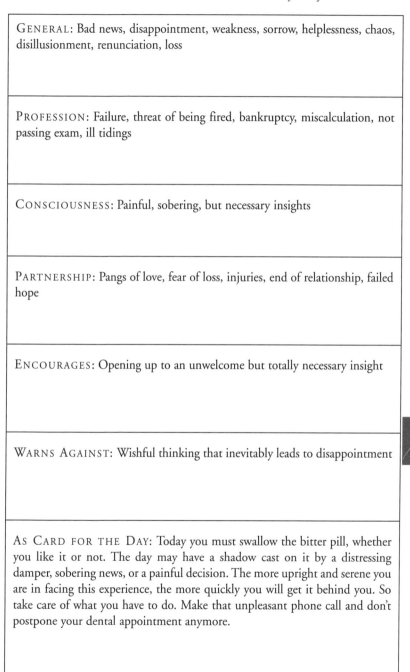

WARNS AGAINST: Wishful thinking that inevitably leads to disappointment

AS CARD FOR THE DAY: Today you must swallow the bitter pill, whether you like it or not. The day may have a shadow cast on it by a distressing damper, sobering news, or a painful decision. The more upright and serene you are in facing this experience, the more quickly you will get it behind you. So take care of what you have to do. Make that unpleasant phone call and don't postpone your dental appointment anymore.

FOUR OF SWORDS
TRUCE

Symbolism	Meaning
St. Andrew's cross	Suffering, martyrdom
Four swords resting on the cross	Standstill that brings neither a change for the worse nor an improvement
Forty-nine petalled rose	Wholeness (7 x 7), love and beauty
Sword tips meet each other at center of flower	Focused mental powers, concentration, pausing
Confused yellow star patterns in background	Restless prospects
Number and Element	Inflexible (4) standpoints (air)
Astrology: Jupiter (♃) in Libra (♎)	Faith/hope (♃) for peace and justice (♎)

GENERAL: Sham peace, temporary retreat, calm before the storm, cowardice, forced break, isolation, building up one's strength

PROFESSION: Stuck situations, job for limited time, short-term work, forced vacation, lack of prospects for future, postponed conflicts

CONSCIOUSNESS: Realization that a truce doesn't mean peace

PARTNERSHIP: Questionable avoidance of conflicts, rethinking the relationship, pause for recovery during crisis in relationship, seeking therapeutic help

ENCOURAGES: Using even a sham peace to work on a genuine solution

WARNS AGAINST: The illusion that everything is fine again

AS CARD FOR THE DAY: Don't trust the peace. A calm doesn't mean that the storm won't break out at any time again. Your problem is only apparently solved, and won't solve itself on its own in the future either. Even if you welcome distractions so you don't have to deal with the annoying topic, it is now actually more important to use the opportunity for finding a genuine solution.

FIVE OF SWORDS
DEFEAT

SYMBOLISM	MEANING
Reversed pentagram of swords and rose petals	Harm, evil, turn for worse
Bent and broken blades	Weakening
Only the most brittle sword points upward	Weak impetus
Destroyed forty-nine petalled rose	Complete destruction, emotional injury
Light in background	The clarity that grows out of failure
Number and Element	Critical (5) perception (air)
Astrology: Venus (♀) in Aquarius (♒)	Willful, unpredictable, frosty (♒) conduct in relationship (♀)

GENERAL: Capitulation, betrayal, humiliation, suffering "shipwreck," vileness

PROFESSION: Failure, disaster, dirty tricks, slander, mobbing, bankruptcy

CONSCIOUSNESS: Understanding that constantly avoiding conflicts practically causes strife

PARTNERSHIP: Spitefulness, hurting each other, vicious power struggles, revenge, divorce, failure

ENCOURAGES: No longer avoiding confrontations, even at the risk of losing this time

WARNS AGAINST: Dangerous developments and projects that are doomed to failure

AS CARD FOR THE DAY: You should develop a "thick skin" today. It may be that you will have to defend yourself against a nasty act of meanness, malicious slander, or dirty tricks. Fight your way through it all as well as you can and remember that even a black Friday is followed by the weekend, during which you can recover. If you recognize where you made your contribution that brought the situation to this point, you may be spared these unpleasant experiences in the future.

SIX OF SWORDS
SCIENCE

SYMBOLISM	MEANING
Six swords form a hexagram	Mutual penetration (six-sided star) of spiritual and earthly world
Tips meet at the center of a yellow rose-cross	Inner striving directed at unity and holistic understanding
Circle in square	The eternal truth (O) concealed in reality (□)
Network and windwheel-like structures	Networked thinking, mental flexibility
Number and Element	Perceptions (air) through combination (6)
Astrology: Mercury (☿) in Aquarius (≈)	Innovative (≈) thinking (☿) and philosophical, scientific (≈) perceiving (☿)

GENERAL: Perception, progress, openness, insight, objectivity, intelligence

PROFESSION: Teamwork, holistic methods of working, freelance business, research, innovative concepts, scientific professions, networked work, invention

CONSCIOUSNESS: Forging ahead to holistic perception

PARTNERSHIP: Equal rights in relationship, trying out something new, kindred souls, clear discussions and agreements

ENCOURAGES: Joy of experimentation and exploration of unknown areas

WARNS AGAINST: Too unreal or too theoretical, soulless concepts

AS CARD FOR THE DAY: Get smart today. Expand your mental horizon by letting yourself be stimulated or specifically get the information that you have long been interested in. Surf the Internet, browse in a bookstore, look through the newspaper for interesting offers, or study the course program at the adult-education center. Perhaps you might even plan an excursion to art and culture. Go to the theater, an exhibition, or an interesting lecture.

SEVEN OF SWORDS
FUTILITY

SYMBOLISM	MEANING
Large sword with Sun symbol	Clear, organizing mind; intellect
Six smaller swords with planetary symbols directed at the large sword	Impairment and threats through illusion (Neptune), stubbornness (Saturn), presumption (Jupiter), destructive frenzy (Mars), falseness (Venus), unscrupulousness (Mercury)
Pale-blue background	Superficiality
Number and Element	Dangerous (7) considerations (air)
Astrology: Moon (☽) in Aquarius (≈)	Changeable, moody (☽) theories and concepts (≈)

GENERAL: Unexpected obstacles, impairment, self-deception, fraud, cowardice

PROFESSION: Murky business deals, being cheated at work, shady practices, obstructionism

CONSCIOUSNESS: Revealing life's lies, failing in one's good intentions

PARTNERSHIP: Dishonesty, hypocrisy, sham harmony, intrigues, inconsistency

ENCOURAGES: Being honest with oneself instead of continuing to pretend about something

WARNS AGAINST: Underestimating outer and inner resistance and already being certain of victory

AS CARD FOR THE DAY: Be on guard. Today your good intentions will be put to the test. If you underestimate your inner resistance and weaknesses, you must reckon with getting stuck in your initial attempts—more likely sooner than later. Moreover, today you tend to kid yourself instead of looking reality in the face. So be wide-awake when dealing with contracts and other agreements. Pay more attention to the fine print than you otherwise would so that you won't be swindled.

EIGHT OF SWORDS
INTERFERENCE

Symbolism	Meaning
Two parallel swords pointing downward, crossed by various scimitars	Willpower and firmness crossed by disruptive influences time and again
Red-violet, jagged background	Revenge, strife, worry
Number and Element	Changeable (8) ideas (air)
Astrology: Jupiter (♃) in Gemini (♊)	High goals (♃) that are threatened by doubts and inner conflicts (♊)

GENERAL: Difficult progress because of distractions, inner conflicts, doubt, absentmindedness, slip-ups, flightiness

PROFESSION: Professional plans are disturbed or sabotaged, unclear areas of competence, unexpected obstacles make the work more difficult

CONSCIOUSNESS: Becoming aware of the disruptive fields that hinder one's own will

PARTNERSHIP: Disagreement about common goals, different needs, standing in each other's way, having difficulty adhering to clear agreements, disruption of relationship through third party

ENCOURAGES: Consistently following one's goal without letting rebounds cause confusion

WARNS AGAINST: Underestimating disruptions and irritations

AS CARD FOR THE DAY: Today you should pay attention to not losing the red thread. Stay persistent and patient. Stand up for your decisions. Even if someone is constantly interrupting, you get caught in traffic, or obstacles are put in your path by an unexpected source, don't let yourself become discouraged. Although such harassing fire may upset your timetable, if you resolutely keep your eye on the goal, you will ultimately achieve it.

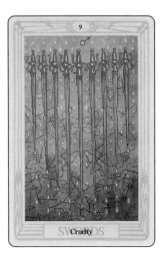

NINE OF SWORDS
CRUELTY

Symbolism	Meaning
Jagged, blood-dripping swords pointed downward	Brutality, raw violence, tyranny
Dripping poison and blood	Poisoned atmosphere, danger
Disorderly pattern in dusky background	Consciousness sinks into the dark areas of primitive affects
Number and Element	Concentration (9) of negative thoughts (air)
Astrology: Mars (♂) in Gemini (♊)	Merciless harshness (♂) and heartless calculating attitude (♊)

GENERAL: Adversity, powerlessness, failure, feelings of guilt, worries, panic

PROFESSION: States of anxiety, not able to meet challenges, suffering because of work situation, being forced to perform a hated task, examination phobia, stage fright

CONSCIOUSNESS: Losing oneself in negative, self-destructive worries or primitive fantasies of violence

PARTNERSHIP: Overpowering fear, heartlessness, pain of separation, emotional cruelty, love-hate relationship, thirst for revenge, shock

ENCOURAGES: Not playing the hero when there is a possibility of sidestepping the problem

WARNS AGAINST: Unpleasant developments and actions that one regrets sooner or later

AS CARD FOR THE DAY: If you are tormenting or plaguing yourself with self-doubts by imagining dreadful scenarios, you should do everything possible to wake up from this nightmare. However, if you actually do see yourself threatened from the outside, there are two possibilities for reacting. Take heart and get it over with, if you must walk this path. However, if there is a true alternative, then you should choose this solution in any case.

TEN OF SWORDS
RUIN

Symbolism	Meaning
Ten swords arranged as the Tree of Life	The totality of the forces
Nine swords destroy the tenth (with the heart hilt)	Raging, destructive forces
Destroyed heart with ten-rayed star	The heart of all ten energy centers of the Tree of Life is destroyed
Reddish yellow background with aggressive structures	Bloody, heated atmosphere
Number and Element	Sum (10) of hostile thoughts (air)
Astrology: Sun (☉) in Gemini (♊)	Fragmentation (♊) of vital force (☉)

GENERAL: Random end, making a clean sweep, putting a stop to something, breakdown, out-of-control destructive energies

PROFESSION: Being suddenly fired, breaking off a professional project, giving up on the work

CONSCIOUSNESS: Insight that something must be broken off

PARTNERSHIP: Breaking up, painful separation, destroying something valuable because of destructive frenzy

ENCOURAGES: Putting an end to something and immediately breaking it off

WARNS AGAINST: Destructive forces and projects doomed to failure

AS CARD FOR THE DAY: Put an end to it. Perhaps you are completely unprepared today to break off or give up something that means a lot to you. However, you also may be very happy because something that has burdened, oppressed, or tormented you for a long time is finally ended. In any case, you should be sure not to let yourself get carried away by destructive frenzy or prematurely throw something overboard that you could regret later.

Princess of Swords

PRINCESS OF SWORDS

Symbolism	Meaning
Battling warrioress	Aggressiveness, impetuous impulsiveness, willingness to engage in conflict
Airy dress	Flexibility
Helmet with head of Medusa	Terror, power
Rotating, transparent wings	Speed, nimbleness
Empty altar on dark smoke clouds	Plundering (which is now being avenged)
Stormy sky	Churned-up mind, restlessness, anger

GENERAL: Young, intellectual woman; female rebel who is nimble-minded and knowledgeable; esprit, clarity, mental renewal, provocation, restlessness, quarrelsome nature

PROFESSION: Conflicts at work, battle for position, clarifying conflict, rebellion

CONSCIOUSNESS: Critical confrontation with old thought patterns

PARTNERSHIP: People with common interests, fighting over standpoints, hateful atmosphere, debates, dirty tricks

ENCOURAGES: Coolly and decisively clarifying a situation

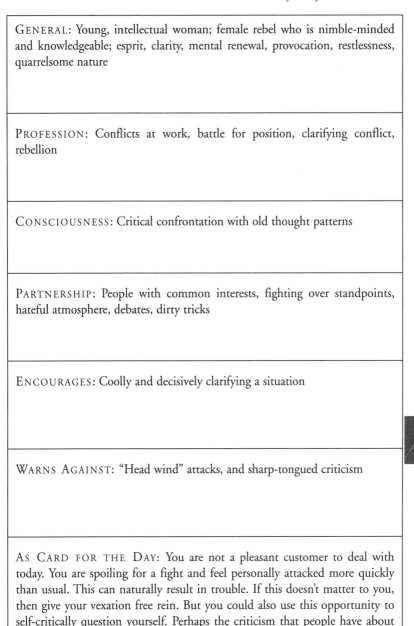

WARNS AGAINST: "Head wind" attacks, and sharp-tongued criticism

AS CARD FOR THE DAY: You are not a pleasant customer to deal with today. You are spoiling for a fight and feel personally attacked more quickly than usual. This can naturally result in trouble. If this doesn't matter to you, then give your vexation free rein. But you could also use this opportunity to self-critically question yourself. Perhaps the criticism that people have about you isn't all that irrelevant and unfounded. If you are willing to listen very precisely, it could very much help you progress on your path.

PRINCE OF SWORDS

Prince of Swords

SYMBOLISM	MEANING
Wildly moving, green male figure in chariot	Flightiness, lack of self-control, inner conflicts, rashness
Green sphere with double pyramid	Power of thought, rationality, analytical spirit
Small, winged figures that draw the chariot in an uncoordinated way	Thoughts running ahead, as yet unorganized ideas of future possibilities
Wings of yellows disks with geometric figures	Inspiring intellect
Sword	Perceptive, constructive mental powers
Sickle	Destructive force
Light, jagged background	Thought fragments, inner conflicts, unsteadiness

GENERAL: The intellectual, the eloquent individual, the technocrat, the position-changer, independence, aimlessness, lightness, slyness, cynicism

PROFESSION: Flightiness, lack of concept, undercooled working climate, flash decision, spaced-out ideas, innovation, quick-wittedness

CONSCIOUSNESS: Intellectual games instead of a search for profound perception

PARTNERSHIP: Cooling down, urge for independence, mood of departure, open or rationally oriented relationship, sharp tongue

ENCOURAGES: Playing with thoughts and curious questioning

WARNS AGAINST: Mental flights of fancy with danger of falling

AS CARD FOR THE DAY: Today you are torn back and forth. You are annoyed because you dissipate your energies, can't reconcile all your ideas, or are snubbed by others as a result. But you may also come across an eloquent person who knows all the tricks of the trade. Don't fall for another's confusing games, and don't let yourself be rattled by cynicism or shadowboxing. It's better to risk conflict in this situation.

Queen of Swords

QUEEN OF SWORDS

Symbolism	Meaning
Woman on mountain of clouds	Peak of perception, clear overview
Sword	Sharp, clear mind
Severed man's head	Liberation from dependencies, mental castration
Crystal crown	Crystallizing ideas, pure intelligence
Child's head as crown ornament	Power of renewal
Deep-blue sky	Benevolent spirit

GENERAL: Wealth of ideas, presence of mind, independence, quick-wittedness; rationally oriented, cultivated, emancipated, critical, clever woman; female individualist

PROFESSION: Negotiating talent, superior independence, brain work, self-reliance, competence, advising or mediating activities

CONSCIOUSNESS: Perceiving one's own dependencies and freeing oneself from them

PARTNERSHIP: Being together in a fair and equal way, practical partnership, passionless relationship, single life, ending a constricting relationship

ENCOURAGES: Reasoning in a crystal-clear manner and proceeding in an independent, skillful, and clever way

WARNS AGAINST: Cynicism and ice-cold calculation

AS CARD FOR THE DAY: Today you could succeed at a true stroke of genius. If you recognize what has kept you self-conscious or trapped up until now, you have a good opportunity of freeing yourself of it for good through a clear decision. But be sure that your approach isn't too radical in your efforts to be independent, since you may inadvertently maneuver yourself into the background. However, an intelligent woman may also be important. Keep an ear open to what she has to tell you.

KNIGHT OF SWORDS

Symbolism	Meaning
Green knight storming forward with sword and dagger	Determined mental powers, astuteness, urge for perception
Golden horse	Highest wisdom, power of perception
Transparent wings turning on the helmet	Flexibility, quickness, agility
Knight and horse as a unity	Powerful connection of mind and instinct
Flying swallows	Goal-oriented thoughts
Stormy, blue-white sky	Aggressiveness

GENERAL: Versatility, discernment, flexibility, intelligence, objectivity, too much emphasis on rational mind, calculation; clever, eloquent, brilliant, goal-oriented man; experienced advisor

PROFESSION: Analytical abilities, business talent, fair team spirit, receiving good advice, making a useful contact, goal-oriented concepts, dynamics; strategic, advisory, or mediating activities

CONSCIOUSNESS: Steering toward new goals while inspired by ideas

PARTNERSHIP: Easy-going but unstable relationship, relationship experiments, very limited will to commit, diversified contacts on a voluntary, non-committal basis

ENCOURAGES: Getting an objective picture of things from a healthy distance

WARNS AGAINST: Letting oneself be guided by theoretical considerations alone

AS CARD FOR THE DAY: Today you shoot straight at your goal. Because you have more convincing concepts and better arguments, which you also present in a charming and witty manner, you can spark enthusiasm for your plans. Above all, you should use this mental clarity where decisions have been pending for a long time. If you have been struggling with a problem for a while, you should get professional advice from a specialist today.

Ace of Disks

ACE OF DISKS

SYMBOLISM	MEANING
Golden coins in the middle of a lively green sphere, inside three rings	New life (3) is created from the union of opposites (1 and 2)
The number 666 at the center	Number of the Great Beast of the Apocalypse
The number 1 above it	Symbol of the "Whore of Babylon," who rides on the Great Beast[6] (her number is 666 + 1 = 667)
ΤΟ ΜΕΓΑ ΘΗΡΙΟΝ (Greek *To Mega Therion* = The Great Beast)	Name of the beast in the Apocalypse, a title that Crowley gave himself
Heptagon surrounded by two intertwined pentagrams, which form the center of a decagon	Holy seal of the order of Astrum Argentum, a magical order that Crowley founded
Number and Element	Enriching (earth) opportunity (Ace = 1)
Astrology: The earth signs: Taurus (♉), Virgo (♍), Capricorn (♑)	Enjoyment (♉), sense of reality (♍), and stability (♑)

[6]See portrayal on Trump card XI = Lust.

GENERAL: Affluence, material happiness, health, inner and outer strength, stability, opportunity for lasting success, sensuality

PROFESSION: Good opportunity for earning money and advancing professionally, secure job, promising business deals

CONSCIOUSNESS: Valuable, enriching experience and perception

PARTNERSHIP: Lasting, solid relationship, physical attraction, enjoyment of sensual pleasures

ENCOURAGES: Using the opportunity to achieve and enjoy something valuable

WARNS AGAINST: A purely materialistic or greedy attitude

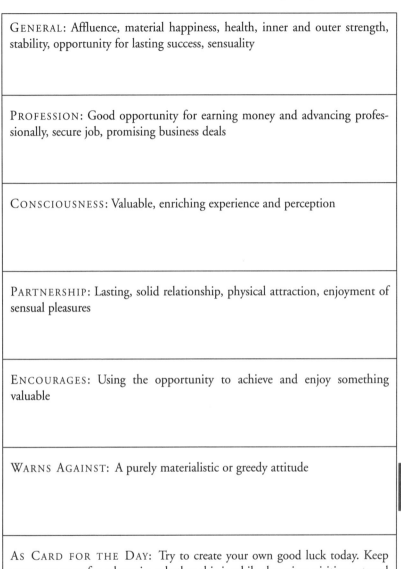

AS CARD FOR THE DAY: Try to create your own good luck today. Keep your eyes open for a bargain, whether this is while shopping, visiting a travel agent, or studying the stock market. Recognize the opportunity that offers itself particularly for all plans and investments that aren't aimed at short-term benefits. Today you can lay the foundation for a project involving long-term prospects that are important to you.

TWO OF DISKS
CHANGE

Symbolism	Meaning
Crowned snake that bites itself in the tail, in the form of an infinity sign and encircling two yin-yang symbols	Eternal exchange and change in tension field of original polarities
Four triangles: symbols of the four elements in their respective color	Change on all levels of being
Violet background	Faith, trust
Number and Element	Interplay (2) of concrete possibilities (earth)
Astrology: Jupiter (♃) in Capricorn (♑)	Expansion (♃) and concentration (♑)

GENERAL: Change, flexible exchange, mutual fructification, variety

PROFESSION: Change of job, restructuring, stabilization of what has been achieved, or new growth after successful consolidation

CONSCIOUSNESS: Insight into the vital rhythm of growth and regression

PARTNERSHIP: Variety in everyday life of relationship, new momentum, changes within a stable relationship, uncommitted flirt

ENCOURAGES: Paying attention to the opposite polarity that has been neglected up until now

WARNS AGAINST: Dissipating one's energies because of inconstancy

As CARD FOR THE DAY: Today you may get into a conflict of interests in which you must juggle apparent contradictions. Remain flexible and stay open for the options. Any kind of one-sidedness will now inevitably lead you to a dead end, in which you will be forced to rethink things because of external circumstances. If, on the other hand, you have more than one iron in the fire, you might even succeed at building a bridge and uniting the previous opposites into one big whole.

THREE OF DISKS
WORKS

Symbolism	Meaning
Light pyramids	Crystallization of creative force
Three red wheels on which the pyramids stand	The powerful trinity of body, mind, and soul produces the visible forms of our three-dimensional world
Troubled ocean in background	Inexhaustible primary potential from which everything is created
Number and Element	Secured, stable (3) values (earth)
Astrology: Mars (♂) in Capricorn (♑)	Forming and processing (♂) matter and reality (♑) with strength (♑) and consistent staying power (♂)

GENERAL: Taking concrete steps, translating ideas into reality, building structures, slow but continuous progress, perseverance, consolidation

PROFESSION: Stabilizing what one has achieved, making progress, turning projects into reality, the developmental phase of profession, creativity, diligence and efficiency, solid work

CONSCIOUSNESS: Striving for secured knowledge

PARTNERSHIP: Building a healthy relationship, stability, mastering everyday life with each other, working together harmoniously

ENCOURAGES: Securing and anchoring what has already been achieved

WARNS AGAINST: Aimless activity

AS CARD FOR THE DAY: You should roll up your sleeves today. It's time to do a proper job and take care of what you have been postponing. This can apply to a variety of areas, such as building a new future for yourself, cultivating the garden, rehabilitating the foundation of your relationship, or putting your finances in order. Clear out what has stood in your way. Persistently turn your program into reality, step-by-step, until you are happy with the results.

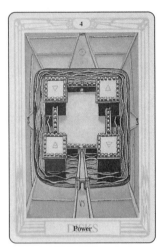

FOUR OF DISKS
POWER

Symbolism	Meaning
Four square towers as corner pillars of a square fortress	Stability, law, structure, and order
Space surrounded by walls and moats	Refuge of security
Balance between the four elements: fire ($\triangle$), air ($\triangleq$), earth ($\triangledown\!\!\!\!-$), and water ($\triangledown$)	Stability, mastery of reality
Number and Element	Enduring (4) security (earth)
Astrology: Sun ($\odot$) in Capricorn (VS)	Self-fulfillment and vitality ($\odot$) through security, structure, and order (VS)

GENERAL: Stability, safeguarding, sense of reality, control, structuring

PROFESSION: Increase of security and power, clear design of concepts, healthy setting of boundaries, mastering problems, creating order, organizational talent

CONSCIOUSNESS: Banking on secured knowledge

PARTNERSHIP: Strengthening relationship, creating clear circumstances, shielding relationship against outer threats

ENCOURAGES: Drawing clear lines and securing what has been achieved

WARNS AGAINST: Having a blockheaded view of the world

AS CARD FOR THE DAY: Today you get control of something that has already annoyed you for a long time. You may put a troublemaker in his or her place, or bring clarity and structure to a confused matter. Don't hesitate to clearly stake off your territory and protect yourself from malevolent, envious, or hostile attacks. Take responsibility and concentrate completely on the things you are in charge of. Wherever it's appropriate, use this day to get something important out of harm's way.

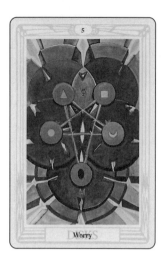

FIVE OF DISKS
WORRY

Symbolism	Meaning
Five disks connected by lines, each with one symbol of the five Tatvas[7] pictured on it	Interplay of forces
The connecting belts form a penta-gram standing on its tip	Connection of bad influences, false direction of goal
Light that shines through the gear system	Good opportunities in the back-ground, concealed by unfavorable development
Number and Element	Material (earth) crisis (5)
Astrology: Mercury (☿) in Taurus (♉)	Bogged-down, obstinate (♉) thinking (☿)

---

[7]Subtle elements that compose reality in Indian philosophy.

GENERAL: Helplessness, fear of loss, constriction, drudgery without results, frustration at nothing working out

PROFESSION: Economic crisis, lack of prospects, insecure position, mobbing, working on ruined projects, hopeless plans

CONSCIOUSNESS: Becoming entangled in nightmares and negative thinking

PARTNERSHIP: Nerve-wracking relationship, having a negative influence on each other, relationship crisis, fears of loss, hurting each other, stubbornly blaming each other in a nasty way

ENCOURAGES: Changing one's ways and taking a new direction

WARNS AGAINST: Becoming increasingly entangled in a hopeless situation

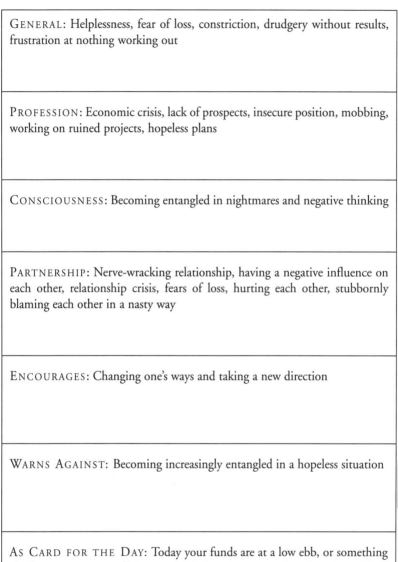

AS CARD FOR THE DAY: Today your funds are at a low ebb, or something else forces you to ease off. In any case, it doesn't appear to be a day where things go easily. If you torment yourself about a bogged-down situation, you shouldn't continue to struggle unnecessarily. Examine things to see whether it's worthwhile to get the stranded ship back on course again. Even if the insight is painful, perhaps it's time to take a new, more promising path that will spare you further frustrations.

SIX OF DISKS
SUCCESS

SYMBOLISM	MEANING
Six-pointed star and hexagon surround a circle of light	Harmonious, lively, fruitful union
Six disks with the symbols of the Moon, Mercury, Venus, Mars, Jupiter, and Saturn in the glow of the Sun	Harmonious interplay of planetary forces in a favorable light
Rose-cross at the center	Spiritual power, inner light
Reddish background	Dawn, sunrise
Number and Element	Successful connection (6) of material values (earth)
Astrology: Moon (☽) in Taurus (♉)	Fertility (☽) and growth (♉), feelings (☽) of abundance and enjoyment (♉)

GENERAL: Increase, material gain, favorable interplay of the forces, welcome development

PROFESSION: Fruitful teamwork, good financial situation, lucrative work, promising new beginning, good planning and coordination

CONSCIOUSNESS: Overcoming inner contradictions and coming to terms with oneself

PARTNERSHIP: Harmony, fruitful relationship, mutual support, happiness in love

ENCOURAGES: Using the favorable preconditions to turn a plan into reality

WARNS AGAINST: Destroying the balance of energy through unreasonable or one-sided expectations

AS CARD FOR THE DAY: This day will be a success. Make a fresh start with united forces, if necessary. You can easily set right whatever has been topsy-turvy or has gone awry up until now—whether this is an annoying assignment, complicated scheduling, or your fitness program. Moreover, when it comes to improving your financial situation, you shouldn't let this day pass without taking advantage of it.

SEVEN OF DISKS
FAILURE

Symbolism	Meaning
Seven leaden Saturn disks on wilted plants	Ruin, weakening, decay
Arrangement of the disks as the geomantic Rubeus figure ⁙	Calamity
Dark, blue-violet background	Shadow world, dying life, chaos
Number and Element	Endangered (7) security (earth)
Astrology: Saturn (♄) in Taurus (♉)	Blockade, end, departure (♄) from possessions and stability (♉)

GENERAL: Destroyed hope, bad circumstances, bad luck, unhappiness, pessimism, loss

PROFESSION: Failure of a project, warning against bad investments, threat of being fired, bankruptcy, unemployment

CONSCIOUSNESS: Insight into the transient and threatening aspects of life

PARTNERSHIP: Morbid times, crisis, fear of loss, failed reconciliation, destruction of relationship

ENCOURAGES: Recognizing futility and turning away from it

WARNS AGAINST: Failures and clinging to something wilted

AS CARD FOR THE DAY: Be careful today—something could go wrong. It's best to postpone things that are really important until tomorrow. Perhaps you might even have to watch something wither and die. Don't try to keep it alive artificially. Its time has run out. The more quickly you understand this, the sooner you will have the opportunity of getting over the related disappointment or crisis.

Prudence

EIGHT OF DISKS
PRUDENCE

SYMBOLISM	MEANING
Eight disks arranged as the geomantic Populus figure ⠿	Winning by not doing anything
Well-rooted tree	Healthy growth
Five-leafed red blossoms shielded by leaves	Powerful fruits are protected as they ripen
Gold-yellow background	Bright perception
Red-green soil	Natural vitality
Number and Element	Careful (earth) new beginning (8)
Astrology: Sun (☉) in Virgo (♍)	Mindful, worldly-wise, prudent (♍) nature (☉)

GENERAL: Cautious new beginning, moderation, skillfulness, care, patience

PROFESSION: Tactically clever way of proceeding, negotiating talent, careful foresight, being able to wait for a favorable opportunity, letting time work for oneself

CONSCIOUSNESS: Deep understanding of natural growth processes

PARTNERSHIP: Cautious new beginning, treating each other carefully, matured relationship, family plans, realistic expectations

ENCOURAGES: A cautious approach to a plan, and letting time work for you

WARNS AGAINST: Immature ideas and premature harvest

AS CARD FOR THE DAY: Lean back and let time work for you. You have a good antenna for what is practical and should calmly plan all further steps. Only impatience, recklessness, or stupidity can prevent good results. So don't let yourself be pressured by circumstances in your environment. Instead, do something for your emotional and physical well-being.

NINE OF DISKS
GAIN

Symbolism	Meaning
Nine disks, of which six are depicted as coins	Solidification and materialization of prospects for success of the Six of Disks card
Upper group with masculine planets Mars (♂), Jupiter (♃), and Saturn (♄)	Outer growth, intellectual striving
Lower group with Mercury (☿) (androgynous) and the feminine planets Moon (☽) and Venus (♀)	Emotional depth, instinctive trust
Middle group with circles and rays in green, red, and blue	Water, fire, and air unite in front of earth-colored background = realization, taking shape
Rich green colors in the background	Fertile ground
Number and Element	Concentration (9) of valuable opportunities (earth)
Astrology: Venus (♀) in Virgo (♍)	Fortuna (♀) brings in the harvest (♍)

GENERAL: Change for the better, well-being, stroke of luck, material increase

PROFESSION: Using lucrative opportunities, worthwhile tasks, welcome changes, raise in pay, professional fulfillment, making a profit

CONSCIOUSNESS: Surprising, enriching perceptions

PARTNERSHIP: Delightful encounter, fulfilling togetherness, joyful developments, happy turn of events

ENCOURAGES: Trusting in one's luck

WARNS AGAINST: Failing to bring in the profit at the right time

AS CARD FOR THE DAY: Be prepared for a pleasant surprise today. Perhaps it will come with the mail, or as an unexpected visitor. Or it may be waiting for you at work. However, it wouldn't do any harm to give luck a chance by becoming active on your own. Take time by the hand and go on a search for the treasure. Do something that you haven't risked doing before, or try out something new. At least buy yourself a lottery ticket!

215

TEN OF DISKS
WEALTH

SYMBOLISM	MEANING
Ten disks depicted as golden coins	Outer wealth
Arrangement in form of Tree of Life[8]	Inner wealth
Magical, Mercurial symbols	Fascination that money holds and a skillful approach to it
Lowest[9] coin is the largest	Danger of placing too much value on the meaning of possessions and getting stuck in material striving
Black-violet disks in the background	Warning against standstill and futility
Number and Element	Abundance (10) of solid values (earth)
Astrology: Mercury (☿) in Virgo (♍)	Cleverness and skill (☿) in business area (♍)

[8] Kabbalistic symbol depicting the totality of Creation.
[9] Lowest position in the Kabbalistic Tree of Life corresponds to Earth.

GENERAL: Solid success, wealth, secure circumstances, having achieved the goal

PROFESSION: Good business deals, optimal working circumstances, successful negotiations, fulfilled everyday working life, security

CONSCIOUSNESS: Becoming aware of one's inner and outer wealth

PARTNERSHIP: Appreciating relationship, stable relationship network, pleasurable togetherness, enjoying a rich relationship

ENCOURAGES: Good business deals and enjoying one's success

WARNS AGAINST: Indolence, and meaningless accumulation of material goods

AS CARD FOR THE DAY: Draw on unlimited resources today. The fruits are just waiting to be plucked. Become aware of your wealth, and allow yourself and others something good. If you are about to conclude a business deal or are offered a favorable opportunity for making money, make use of today for this purpose. Whatever you tackle has the tendency to turn into hard cash!

PRINCESS OF DISKS

SYMBOLISM	MEANING
Pregnant woman	Creative force
Luminous crystal tip	Crystalline light born from dark matter
Spear penetrating the earth	Physical union of masculine and feminine energy
Cape of sheepskin, ram's horns	Closeness to nature, original wildness
Rose of the goddess Isis with yin-yang symbol	Harmonious combination of feminine and masculine archetypal energies that brings forth beauty and new life
Trees reaching up into the sky with roots of light	The holy grove that connects Heaven and Earth

GENERAL: Young, sensual, fertile woman; naturalness, creativity, growth, pregnancy

PROFESSION: Work in nature or for nature, practical activities, crafts, work with animals or plants, lucrative prospects, creativity

CONSCIOUSNESS: Willingness to let oneself be "fructified"

PARTNERSHIP: Sensual relationship, warm love, long-term fruitful relationship, addition to the family, building something together

ENCOURAGES: Accepting a fructifying impulse and creatively translating it into reality

WARNS AGAINST: Becoming one-sided or fixated on material values

AS CARD FOR THE DAY: Today you are standing on the basis of the facts. Solid tasks are more appealing than glittering, speculative ideas. With your sense for practical solutions, you can easily succeed in bringing order to your everyday life. In case you have neglected the garden work or handicraft tasks lately, you will enjoy taking care of these things today. In addition, you have the desire to enjoy life sensually. Take enough time for this and seize a good opportunity when it comes along.

PRINCE OF DISKS

Prince of Disks

Symbolism	Meaning
Naked man on a span of oxen with a bull's head on the helmet	Earthy power, sensuality
Globe with circles and square figure at the center	World of visible manifestation, structures of cyclic order
Scepter	Culmination of the work
Concentric circles in background	Cycles of the seasons
Ears of grain and flowers	Fertility, closeness to nature
Fruits on the wagon	Fertility and potency

GENERAL: Energetic young man, prime mover, person with imperturbable staying power ("steamroller"), sense of reality, persistence, endurance, concentration, initiative

PROFESSION: Consistently working toward a goal that has been set, business abilities, worthwhile activities, long-term employment, agriculture and gardening

CONSCIOUSNESS: Sharpening one's sense of reality

PARTNERSHIP: Stability, intense sensual experiences, commitment, feeling secure, developing something together

ENCOURAGES: Seeing things through and turning one's goals into reality with endurance and consistency

WARNS AGAINST: Unimaginative delusions about what's feasible; pigheadedness

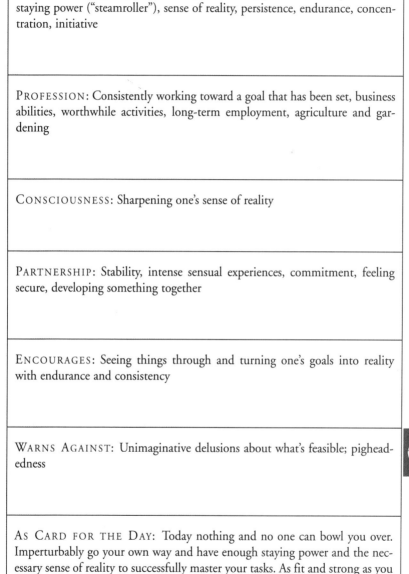

AS CARD FOR THE DAY: Today nothing and no one can bowl you over. Imperturbably go your own way and have enough staying power and the necessary sense of reality to successfully master your tasks. As fit and strong as you feel, you certainly won't avoid any test of strength! But, even more, you would welcome an opportunity for some pleasurable sensual delight that you could completely enjoy.

QUEEN OF DISKS

Queen of Disks

SYMBOLISM	MEANING
Woman on pineapple throne	Queen of fertility, Mother Earth
Armor of coins	Security, sense of material values
Curved giant horns as headdress	Instinctual power, vitality, libido
Scepter with crystal pointing upward	Clear perception, connection of spirit and matter
Sphere with overlapping circles	Eternal cycle of dying and becoming
Desert with river in background	Meagerness and loneliness that have been overcome
Ram on globe	Representative of persistence of earth elements

GENERAL: Fertility, sense of security, sensuality, serenity, endurance; a mature, experienced woman; being calm, patient, stable, trustworthy

PROFESSION: Willingness to assume responsibility, worthwhile projects, strong character

CONSCIOUSNESS: Patiently trusting in the natural life cycles

PARTNERSHIP: Trusting each other, perseverance, mature relationship, loyalty, starting a family, sense of security

ENCOURAGES: Dedicating oneself to concrete tasks with endurance and patience

WARNS AGAINST: Meaningless drudgery and unimaginative striving for possessions

AS CARD FOR THE DAY: Don't let yourself become confused or put under pressure today. Whatever you have planned, do it in a leisurely and calm manner. You know that good wine only matures with the years. So keep your long-term goal in mind and cultivate your fields with patience and care so that they provide a rich harvest. It may also be possible that a motherly woman with a natural, sensual charisma becomes important for you today. Trust in her advice.

Knight of Disks

KNIGHT OF DISKS

SYMBOLISM	MEANING
Knight on stocky, standing horse	Connection to the earth, instinctual nature, sense of reality, unyieldingness
Black armor	Security
Red saddle	Activity, instinctive nature, and creative, procreative potential
Flail, ripe grain	Harvest, fertility
Pushed-back helmet with stag's head	Expanded perception, openness to spiritual aspects
Black shield surrounded by luminous circles	Creative spirit connects with matter

GENERAL: Firmness, sobriety, perseverance, stable values, reliability, straightforwardness; mature, sensual man; realist, pragmatist, guarantee of security

PROFESSION: Responsible position, business talent, uncompromising approach, good business deals, secured income, practical abilities, solid sense for property

CONSCIOUSNESS: Becoming aware of the responsibility that results from possessions

PARTNERSHIP: Stable relationship, sensuality, mutual appreciation, trust

ENCOURAGES: Enjoying what has been achieved and using one's means and possibilities in a responsible manner

WARNS AGAINST: Stubbornness and meaningless hoarding

AS CARD FOR THE DAY: Today you should look at the fruits of your efforts and enjoy the success. Be aware of your wealth and rest a bit on your laurels. But if, in the process, you get some ideas about what plans you would like to realize next, this is a good sign. But it's just as good and important in the coming time period to persistently secure what you have achieved. Perhaps a man, who you recognize by his very good-natured but sober manner, will become important for you. Listen to his advice or accept his suggestions.

SAMPLE
INTERPRETATIONS

Example 1

 n the basis of The Plan Game layout, the following example shows how the interpretive texts in this book can be used to read the cards.

The asker had been in a deep emotional crisis for a long time. She wanted to use the cards to find out what she should do to find joy in life. She drew the following cards:

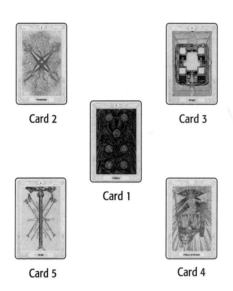

Card 2   Card 3

Card 1

Card 5   Card 4

THE INTERPRETATION:

1st card = Significator = Seven of Disks (Failure)

The significator provides important information for the question. In view of the theme, we should look under the heading of "Consciousness" to learn the meaning of the Seven of Disks. There we find: "Insight into transient and threatening aspects of life."

2nd card = The force driving the asker = Two of Wands (Dominion)

In addition to the encouraging statement, "Eagerness to fight, courage, and willingness to take risks" as the general meaning of the card, the heading "Consciousness" is also important. Here it says: "Recognizing destructive processes as the precondition for creative phases."

3rd card = Outer objections or encouragement = Four of Disks (Power)

The asker experiences stability and structure, as well as perhaps control, from the outside world.

4th card = This is how it will not succeed = Prince of Wands

The Prince of Wands shows what the asker shouldn't do, the approach that won't allow her to succeed in overcoming her depression. This card's meaning can be read under the heading "Warns Against": "Spontaneous satisfaction of desires at expense of long-term goals."

5th card = This is how it will succeed = Five of Wands (Strife)

On the other hand, she will master her crisis by following the suggestion made by the Five of Wands. Its meaning can be read under the heading "Encourages": "Risking something new and facing the competition."

OVERVIEW OF THE READING:

The chances seem good. The initial card (Failure) shows the source of this crisis very clearly. Fortunately, the driving force (Dominion) is strong. The support from outside (Power) is positive and stabilizing, and the warning (Prince of Wands) that short-term pleasure gains will not bring a solution, is extremely illuminating. The guiding advice (Strife) immediately makes sense to the asker; this challenge to be willing to risk something new additionally receives valuable support through the 2nd card (Dominion), which shows that the asker inwardly feels pushed in exactly that direction.

QUINTESSENCE

The sum of all the cards is 18 and therefore leads to The Moon (XVIII) and The Hermit (IX) as the quintessence. This means that the concluding advice of the tarot is: "Take the path of fear in a cautious but decisive manner. Look for the silver lining (Moon). While doing so, don't let yourself be influenced or irritated by anyone, but stay true to yourself (Hermit)."

Example 2

The next example shows how unambiguous the tarot can be when asked decision questions. The asker, who had already commuted for years between Vienna and Munich, laid The Decision Game spread in order to learn whether he should move in with his girlfriend in Munich at some point during the next twelve months. The cards responded as follows:

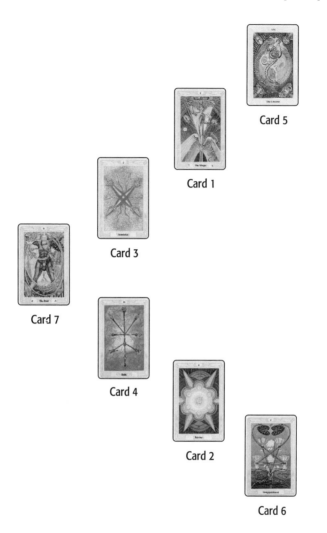

Card 5

Card 1

Card 3

Card 7

Card 4

Card 2

Card 6

THE INTERPRETATION:

7th card = Significator = The Fool

"New beginning" and "starting off into the unknown" are among the key words for this card. This isn't surprising in view of the question. In terms of one's profession, The Fool can mean "starting at zero," but on the level of partnership it can represent "feelings of spring." The asker could easily connect all of these themes with a possible move.

The 3rd, 1st, and 5th cards show what will happen if he moves to Munich.

3rd card = Two of Wands (Dominion)

Courage and a willingness to take risks are at the beginning of this path. As a professional consequence of the move, this card means facing new challenges. On the personal level, in addition to a highly charged atmosphere, it may also mean some friction and struggling for position.

1st card = The Magus

He shows mastery on all levels and therefore reveals that the beginning challenges will soon be handled in a skillful way.

5th card = The Universe

The meaning of "being at the right place" and the fact that The Universe is also a signal card[1] makes it clear that the long-term prospects are also extremely good. These cards clearly point to Munich in an unmistakable manner. It could hardly be more clear. (Incidentally, in order to counter the possible skepticism of some doubters, these cards were authentically laid in this manner. This is not an imaginary example!)

The 4th, 2nd, and 6th cards show what will happen if he stays in Vienna.

4th card = Ten of Swords (Ruin)

The end or break that this card signifies can have a number of meanings. A typical meaning for the Ten of Swords in this position is that the failure of the upper path will be experienced as an arbitrary, if not even brutal, step. However, it can also mean that the lower path cannot be taken without difficulty but begins with a sudden clash. This would correspond to an unexpected or involuntary event in Vienna. Moreover, the card could also warn that the decision against Munich would result in the failure of the relationship. But the next card makes this interpretation seem unlikely.

2nd card = Six of Disks (Success)

"Harmonious interplay of the forces," means that welcome developments will occur in Vienna after an initial hardship. However—in view of the following cards—these will not last long.

6th card = Five of Cups (Disappointment)

The lower path means nothing good in the long run. It is headed for disappointed expectations, disappearing hopes, and painful perceptions.

---

[1] See page 45.

SUMMARY AND QUINTESSENCE:

In addition to the clear recommendation of taking the more promising path and moving to Munich, the cards also give an indication of how this decision should be made. As a quintessence, their sum (45) leads to The Hermit, whose advice is: "Go within yourself to find out what you really want. Don't let yourself be influenced by anyone. Collect your forces before you risk the step into something new."

Glossary

Arcana: Plural of the Latin word *Arcanum* = secret. Name for all the tarot cards, which are subdivided into the major and minor arcana.

Ace: The first card of each suit, which corresponds to the number 1.

Color Suits: The four suits of the minor arcana, consisting respectively of 14 cards with the same symbols (Wands, Cups, Swords, or Disks).

Court Cards: Princess, Prince, Queen, and Knight. The cards of the Minor Arcana named according to the court of the King.

Cup: The tarot symbol corresponding to the water element.

Deck: A complete tarot set with 78 cards.

Disk: The tarot symbol corresponding to the earth element. Also called Coins or Pentacles in other tarot decks.

Major Arcana: The 22 cards, also called trumps, that show individual motifs and bear a name (The Fool, The Magus, The High Priestess, etc.) These are numbered from 0 to XXI.

Minor Arcana: The 56 cards that include the four color suits (Wands, Cups, Swords, and Disks) of 14 cards each.

Number Cards: The ten cards of each color suit, numbered from 1 to 10, whereby the Ace corresponds with the 1.

Quintessence: The concluding advice when the cards are laid. Result of adding all the cards that have been turned over. (See page 28)

Reversed Cards: Cards that are uncovered upside-down while laying the cards. Some card-readers attribute a different meaning to them than when the cards turned over in the proper direction. (See page 27)

Significator: The card at the center in "The Relationship Game" or "The Decision Game," for example. It shows the current status of the relationship or question being asked. In addition, some card-readers use this as a symbol of the asker's selected card, which is laid next to the cards or beneath the first card, at the start of laying the cards.

Suits: *See* Color Suits.

Sword: The tarot symbol corresponding to the air element.

Trump Cards: *See* Major Arcana.

Upside-Down Cards: *See* Reversed Cards.

Wand: The tarot symbol corresponding to the fire element.

Selected Bibliography

Akron and Hajo Banzhaf. *The Crowley Tarot*, Christine M. Grimm, trans. Stamford: U.S. Games, 1995.

Banzhaf, Hajo. *The Tarot Handbook*, Christine M. Grimm, trans. Stamford: U.S. Games, 1993.

———. *Tarot and the Journey of the Hero*, Christine M. Grimm, trans. York Beach, ME: Samuel Weiser, 2000.

Banzhaf, Hajo and Anne Haebler. *Key Words for Astrology*, Christine M. Grimm, trans. York Beach, ME: Samuel Weiser, 1996.

Banzhaf, Hajo and Brigitte Theler. *Secrets of Love and Partnership*, Christine M. Grimm, trans. York Beach, ME: Samuel Weiser, 1998.

Becker, Udo. *Lexikon der Symbole*. Freiburg: Herder, 1992.

Biedermann, Hans. *Dictionary of Symbolism: Cultural Icons and the Meanings Behind Them.* New York: Meridian, 1994.

Bürger, Evelin and Johannes Fiebig. *Tarot: Spiegel Deiner Möglichkeiten.* Trier: Kleine Schritte, 1991.

Cooper, J. C. *An Illustrated Encyclopedia of Traditional Symbols.* London: Thames & Hudson, 1978.

Crowley, Aleister. *The Book of Thoth.* York Beach, ME: Samuel Weiser, 1969.

Franz, Marie-Louise von.Krefting, Miki. *Einführung in den Crowley-Tarot.* Neuhausen: Urania, 1992.

Luft, Joseph. *Group Processess: An Introduction to Group Dynamics.* Palo Alto, CA: Mayfield Publishing, 1970.

Miers, Horst E. *Lexikon des Geheimwissens.* Munich: Goldmann, 1987.

Tegtmeier, Ralph. *Aleister Crowley, Die tausend Masken des Meisters.* Munich: Knaur, 1989.

von Franz, Marie-Louise. *Individuation in Fairy Tales.* Boston: Shambhala, 1990.

Ziegler, Gerd. *Tarot: Mirror of the Soul.* York Beach, ME: Samuel Weiser, 1988.

Index

HAJO BANZHAF has been writing, lecturing, and working with the tarot and astrology since the early 1980s. He presents tarot seminars in Europe on a regular basis. His articles appear in well-known European magazines. He also served as the editor of the Kailash Book Series published by Hugendubel, an old and respected German esoteric publishing house. He has written 12 books, including *The Tarot and the Journey of the Hero*, recently published by Weiser. His first USA appearance, in Chicago, takes place at the International Tarot Conference in September, 2001. Some readers may want to explore his website at www.maja.com.HajoBanzhaf.htm.

BRIGITTE THELER also has a background in astrology and the tarot. She is the editor of *Astrologie Heute* [Astrology Today] and coauthored, with Hajo Banzhaf, *The Secrets of Love and Partnership*, an astrology title also published by Weiser. She lives in Zurich, Switzerland.